Beyond Atkins

ABOUT THE AUTHOR

Dr. Douglas J. Markham is the author of *Total Health* and *Low-Carb Cocktails* and the founder of www.totalhealthdoc.com, an online weight loss and wellness management system that has helped thousands of people lose weight and achieve a healthy lifestyle. He has appeared on CNN's *Larry King Live,* where he announced the launch of his HEALTH Across America Tour, a national obesity prevention public education campaign that targeted America's twenty-five "fattest cities." He lives in Southern California.

PRAISE FOR DR. DOUG

"My family and I follow [his] well-balanced principles."

—John Schneider,
actor-director and star of the WB television series *Smallville*

"I'm a personal believer in his well-balanced approach. . . . Dr. Doug helped me take off the few extra pounds I had gained after my second child!"

—Dr. Marleece Barber, physician and medical director
of Lockheed Martin Space Systems/NASA

"[His] Total Health program can literally help save people's lives!"

—Dr. Henry Heimlich, physician-humanitarian, developer of the
Heimlich maneuver, and founder of the Heimlich Institute

"[I]nformative and dynamic. . . . Dr. Doug [has] helped many of our employees gain control of their health."

—Barbara Essie, wellness chairman, American Family Insurance Group

Eat, drink, and be healthy with Dr. Doug—and raise a glass to
Low-Carb Cocktails
Now available from Pocket Books

Also by Dr. Douglas J. Markham

Total Health
Low-Carb Cocktails

Available from Pocket Books

Beyond Atkins

*A Healthier, More Balanced Approach
to a Low-Carbohydrate Way of Eating*

Featuring Total Health Menu Options, Recipes,
and the 30-Minute "Fat-Burning" Circuit Training Workout

Dr. Douglas J. Markham

**Best-Selling Author and Founder of the Total Health
Weight Loss and Wellness Management System**

Foreword by Larry King
Author and Host of CNN'S *Larry King Live*

POCKET BOOKS

New York London Toronto Sydney

First published in Great Britain by Pocket Books, 2005
An imprint of Simon & Schuster UK Ltd
A Viacom Company

3 5 7 9 10 8 6 4

Simon & Schuster UK Ltd
Africa House
64–78 Kingsway
London WC2B 6AH

www.simonsays.co.uk

Simon & Schuster Australia
Sydney

A CIP catalogue record for this book is available from the British Library.

ISBN 1-4165-0228-9
EAN 9781416502289

Printed and bound in Great Britain by Cox & Wyman Ltd, Reading, Berkshire

Care has been taken to ensure the accuracy of the information presented herein and to describe generally accepted practices. However, the author, editor, and publisher are not responsible for errors or omissions or for any consequences from the application of the information in this book and make no warranty, express or implied, with regard to the contents of the book.

Further, as new scientific information becomes available through basic and clinical research and studies, recommended treatments and procedures undergo changes. Thus, although the author, editor, and publisher have done everything reasonably possible to make this book accurate and up to date, current procedures, methods, and practices are dynamic and subject to change. In addition, individual anatomy, physiology, requirements, and capabilities vary, and specific recommendations applicable in general may not be appropriate for a particular individual. Lastly, this book is not intended to be taken as medical advice nor to supplant appropriate medical consultation but rather is intended to be educational. In view of all of the foregoing, the reader is therefore advised to always consult with his or her physician or other appropriate health and fitness professional regarding these matters.

Acknowledgments

I want to express my gratitude to the many people who made this book possible, starting with my patients, staff, and friends, who urged me to share the Total Health weight loss and wellness program with the rest of the world. This book would not exist without their unwavering support. In particular, I'd like to thank the people whose time, talent, and dedication helped shape and polish the pages that follow.

My deepest gratitude goes to Larry King, author, show host, and founder of the Larry King Cardiac Foundation, who, despite the enormous demands made upon him, found the time to contribute an eloquent and thoughtful foreword expressing the importance of taking control of your health. He has always been a special source of inspiration and encouragement to all of us through his fair and balanced approach to covering our world's events.

Henry Heimlich, M.D., developer of the Heimlich maneuver, founder of the Heimlich Institute, humanitarian, and fellow Rotarian, for his review of this manuscript and, much more important, his contributions to the human race. His life's contributions have probably saved more lives than the efforts of any other individual in the history of humankind through his innovative lifesaving techniques.

Thanks to U.S. Secretary of Health Tommy Thompson and our surgeon general, Richard Carmona, M.D., for their administration's commitment to fighting obesity. Also to Tommy Thompson's and my fine home state of Wisconsin, for providing us with a wholesome environment and an excellent public education system during our childhood years.

A special thanks to my good friend John Schneider, actor and director, whose inspirational story of overcoming childhood obesity has inspired millions of people. Also for his enthusiasm and support of me and my efforts to enlighten society about the pitfalls of obesity-related diseases.

Thanks also to Frank M. Dawson, M.D., family practitioner, for his continued friendship and his tireless commitment to his patients and community service work with the Conejo Free Clinic.

A big thank-you to my friend Jackson Sousa, exercise physiologist and personal trainer, for his review of the exercise section of this book and for getting me into shape as my personal trainer.

Thank you to Cynthia Langford, registered dietician, for her support and review of the nutritional concepts that make the Total Health protein-rich, favorable-carbohydrate way of eating a well-balanced success.

Thanks to Stephen G. Axelrode, D.O., family practice, chief of primary care, Los Robles Regional Medical Center; Miguel Gonzalez, M.D., internal medicine; and Mel Hayashi, M.D., orthopedist; for their patient referrals and professional feedback.

I am also grateful to Troy Leinen, manager of human resources, and Karen Lehman, R.N., occupational health services, of Bombardier Aerospace/Learjet, for supporting Total Health as an employee benefit and Internet-based corporate wellness program.

Thanks to Robert Shaw, chief executive officer, Los Robles Regional Medical Center, for helping me introduce the Total Health program to the medical community, and to his wife, Lisa, who has championed Total Health's benefits to youth through local Parent-Teacher Associations.

Thanks to Tom Voccola and Frances Fujii, cofounders of CEO², for their support, friendship, and corporate visioning principles, which have helped shape and polish my life's purpose, goals, and dreams.

Multitudes of gratitude must be given to Anna Moses, public relations manager of the Dannon Company, Inc., and to Gerry Morrison, president/chairman of the board, and Roeland Polet, chief executive officer, Carbolite Foods, Inc., for their belief in the Total Health program and their company's monetary support, moral support, and continued commitment to the Health Across America campaign.

Huge praise to Carol Marriot, executive director of the Ventura County Western States Affiliate of the American Heart Association and to the American Heart Association and its volunteers for their tireless efforts in enlightening the public in the prevention of heart disease and stroke. Also for her vision and humanitarian efforts to serve the underserved Hispanic population of Ventura County.

A special thanks to Alan M. Horwitz for his midwestern values, ethics, and legal direction throughout this project. Also to his wife, JoAnne Horwitz, for her huge heart—no pun intended—for her volunteer efforts with the American Heart Association in educating women about the leading causes of death in women, which are heart disease and stroke.

Thanks to David H. Murdock, chairman and chief executive officer of Dole Food Company, Inc., for his commitment to providing the finest-quality fresh fruit and vegetable products on the planet. Also for his vision in publishing the *Encyclopedia of Foods,* the finest and most comprehensive reference book on general health that I've ever seen.

A heartfelt thanks goes to Simon & Schuster's Louise Burke, publisher; Liate Stehlik, vice president of publishing/associate publisher; and Christina E. Boys, associate editor, for their editorial direction and boundless enthusiasm for this program and its ability to change people's lives.

Contents

PART III
Eating Your Way to Total Health

PART IV
Exercise: How to Get Started and Why

PART V
Mental Health: Helpful Hints for Happiness

PART VI
Total Health Recipes

Foreword

Dr. Doug Markham is an incredible young man. I first met him when he was a guest on my television show and found his thoughts and presentation most impressive.

I then received an advance copy of his book, *Beyond Atkins: A Healthier, More Balanced Approach to a Low-Carbohydrate Way of Eating*. It is certainly among the best printed material ever about the subject of good health, diabetes control, and balanced living.

I've lost weight, and my blood sugar level is generally below 100, which is remarkable for someone with type 2 diabetes, which I have. I have reduced the amount of supportive prescription medications I've been taking, and I'm on my way to eliminating them completely.

His exercise program makes a lot of sense and isn't difficult.

If you follow Dr. Doug's advice, I can almost guarantee that you will lead a better, healthier life.

Go get 'em!

Larry King

Larry King and Dr. Doug

Preface

The idea behind the Total Health program is that you have the absolute right to health and happiness. You work hard to provide for yourself and your loved ones. Compromise and sacrifice are part of life. Unfortunately, it's all too easy to compromise your physical and mental health along the way.

And that's a crime. Because if you've sacrificed your health, you'll end up spending your hard-earned resources on medical bills, trying to counteract a lifetime of poor health choices. It's hard to enjoy the fruits of your labor when the lifestyle you've worked so hard to achieve is limited by deteriorated health.

The Total Health program has inspired and enlightened individuals to achieve optimum health and wellness by combining a protein-rich, favorable-carbohydrate way of eating with regular physical exercise, intellectual development, and spiritual growth.

Thousands of people have participated in the Total Health program, with many of them no longer needing prescription medications for diseases such as high blood pressure, high cholesterol, and adult-onset diabetes.

It's my sincere belief that everyone has the absolute right to be both healthy and happy. People just need the right tools to help empower them to effect change.

In July 2002, John Schneider and I appeared together on CNN's *Larry King Live,* where John shared his struggle with childhood obesity for the first time on national television. There I announced my plans to depart on my HEALTH Across America Tour, part of a national public education campaign on the prevention of obesity-related diseases. This tour will eventually take me to America's twenty-five "fattest" cities, as ranked by *Men's Fitness* magazine.

Dr. Doug's and John Schneider's appearance on CNN's Larry King Live

At age 16, with a 44-inch waist, a height of six feet, three inches, and weighing just under 250 pounds, John heeded the advice of his brother and began making lifestyle changes. Two years and 50 pounds later, John's acting career took him to the top when he was cast as heartthrob Bo Duke on television's *The Dukes of Hazzard*. John currently stars on the WB hit television series *Smallville* and subscribes to the Total Health weight loss and wellness management philosophy.

John Schneider before

John Schneider before

John Schneider after

The idea for an expanded version of my first book, *Total Health,* resulted from the overwhelming response to John's inspirational story and my continued commitment to fighting childhood and adult obesity. The goal of this book is to enlighten the world with a simple, safe, and effective answer to gaining control of your weight loss, wellness, and fitness goals.

The solution to our present health and obesity epidemic will require effective collaboration among government, volunteer organizations (the American Heart Association, PTAs, etc.), and the private sector (media, TV, radio, print, etc.), as well as a commitment to action by parents, individuals, and communities to provide a simple approach through proper *education, implementation,* and *follow-up.*

Remember, it's your absolute right to be healthy and happy! It's my sincere and deepest desire that this book and the Total Health program helps you take your first steps toward taking control of your health and creating a lifetime of health and happiness!

Yours in Total Health,
Dr. Doug

P.S. Even though the Total Health program is a much more balanced approach to a *low-carbohydrate way of eating,* I must give thanks to the pioneers of protein-based diets—people such as Dr. Stillman, Dr. Atkins, and others, who, despite the ridicule of their peers and the nutritional establishment, remained true to their beliefs. They were always on the right track, but their approaches were just not well balanced enough for a long-term health approach.

Beyond Atkins

Part I

Why the Total Health Plan Works

THE BIRTH OF TOTAL HEALTH

Several years before I started my Total Health program in 1996, I had the unique opportunity as a doctor of chiropractic to work in a medical office with doctors who specialized in family practice. We referred a number of patients to one another. Many of our "shared" patients suffered from problems caused by obesity, such as high blood pressure, high cholesterol, and diabetes, conditions that they preferred to address through lifestyle changes in diet and exercise rather than medication.

So the M.D.s recommended a low-fat, high-carbohydrate diet and exercise program, an approach that was popular in the 1980s and early 1990s, which I too followed. But there was a problem. It wasn't working!

Even though our patients were following the classic low-fat, high-carbohydrate nutritional guidelines promoted by the health care community, they were not losing much weight. They were not regulating their blood sugar levels. They were not lowering their cholesterol or reducing their blood pressure.

In the mid-1990s, I began to have some health problems of my own—namely, I couldn't keep my energy levels up. I've always been a very active person. In high school, I was an All-American wrestler. And as a doctor, I loved cross-training for triathlons.

So I was riding my bike, swimming, and running. I was also training a couple mornings a week in a form of Brazilian jujitsu. I was taking my supplements. And I was on my high-carb, low-fat diet. When it came to training and nutrition, I was doing everything right. I figured I should be a superhuman. Instead I was exhausted.

I'd have my high-carb meal, pasta with low-fat red sauce and some veggies, and about half an hour later, I felt as though I needed to take a nap.

I knew something was wrong. I even had my blood tested to see if I had anemia.

I then became aware of nutritional principles popularized by best-selling books such as *Enter the Zone* by Barry Sears, Ph.D., and *Protein Power* by Michael Eades, M.D., and Mary Eades, M.D. According to these books, you could increase your energy levels by regulating your blood sugars.

The key was to eat protein-rich, favorable-carbohydrate meals—not eliminate all carbohydrates, just increase the protein and ease off the unfavorable forms of carbohydrates.

So I decided to give the Zone a try. For one thing, the physiology behind this way of eating made sense. For another, this was a balanced approach to eating, not some extreme alternative such as diet pills or liquid meals.

The results were fantastic. Within about two weeks my energy levels soared. I also lost about five pounds around the middle. Remember, all I wanted was more energy. The weight loss was a bonus! Most of all, I was excited about the prospect of sharing this information with my patients.

But unfortunately, I couldn't tell my patients to go out and buy these books because they were too technical for most people to understand. So I did more research and used my personal experience to make this exciting information accessible and easy to use in the real world.

The dramatic results I began to see in my patients were nothing short of life-changing. Patients who were obese have lost the weight. In many cases, their M.D.s have taken them off their high blood pressure medications, their diabetes medications, and their cholesterol medications. And the weight has stayed off. Total Health is not some fad diet. It's a way of eating that will work for the rest of your life.

WHY OTHER DIETS DON'T WORK

Much of what has been written about the nutritional principles behind eating a diet with more protein and less carbohydrates is too technical, not totally effective, or not well balanced.

Dr. Sears did a great job of verifying the scientific basis of how and why a protein-rich, favorable-carbohydrate way of eating is healthier and much more effective than the classic low-fat, high-carbohydrate diet in his book

Enter the Zone. Unfortunately, the information in the book was too technical for many readers to understand and implement in their own lives.

The other problem is that Dr. Sears is a research scientist and never actually had his own weight loss/wellness clinic. His program is based on the 40-30-30 concept. This represents the amount of carbohydrates, protein, and fat a person should eat at each meal or snack. He suggests 40 percent carbohydrates, 30 percent protein, and 30 percent fat.

What I have observed with patients who have come to my office following the Zone program is that they usually lose some weight and feel better, but they often do not reach their target weight loss goals. They may lose 20 or 30 pounds and still have 10 to 20 more pounds to go. This leads to frustration, and many times they abandon the program. The reason for this plateau in weight loss is that they are not limiting their carbohydrate intake enough to get the job done.

The Atkins plan, on the other hand, as outlined in *Dr. Atkins' New Diet Revolution* suggests limiting your carbohydrate intake a lot more. This is good for rapid weight loss, but many health care providers feel that the weight loss can be *too* rapid. Burning fat too fast can lead to a condition called *ketosis*. The by-product of burning fat is *ketones,* which accumulate in the body and pass through our kidneys before being excreted in the urine. Passing ketones in large quantities too rapidly is thought to be potentially damaging to the kidneys.

The Atkins plan also suggests eliminating fruits as a carbohydrate choice from your diet during the "induction phase" of the program. This suggestion, along with allowing people to disregard portion control and the fat content of their daily protein choices, has led to skepticism that it is a balanced approach to weight loss and long-term health.

Even though the Atkins plan works for weight loss in the short term, it doesn't appear to be well balanced enough for the long term. This is also where I'm in agreement with the majority of cardiologists and the nutritional establishment: I want people to choose healthier protein options, and I don't want them to disregard the fat content of their meals.

I also allow fiber-rich fruits in the weight loss stages as long as they're on the low-glycemic "Macronutrient Units" list (page 85) in the "Eating Your Way to Total Health" section of this book. Fruits are healthier carbohydrate choices that contain essential nutrients and fiber, and won't inhibit weight loss as long as they're not consumed in excessive amounts.

The other point that separates the Total Health plan from the Atkins plan is portion control. We need to base the amount of protein we eat at each meal on the size of our body frames. This is called your *daily protein requirement*. This is also outlined in the "Eating Your Way to Total Health" section.

Arthur Agatston, a Florida cardiologist, did a better job of addressing the importance of fat content in his book *The South Beach Diet*, but, like the Atkins plan, his diet eliminates fruit from the initial phase.

The South Beach plan also suggests "normal-size" portions, but it doesn't address the definition of what is "normal size" for a given individual's body frame size. Therefore, anyone trying to follow the plan is left wondering how much he or she should eat at each meal. This, once again, can potentially lead to portion control issues.

Another very important component that seems to be left out of most plans such as Atkins and South Beach is a definitive exercise program. Many of these plans make reference to the importance of exercise but fail to give their readers or followers an actual step-by-step plan to incorporate into their busy lives.

That's why I dedicate a whole section to how to get started on an exercise program as well as providing a comprehensive, easy-to-implement circuit training exercise regime that can be performed at home, in the office, or while traveling.

The new, balanced approach to a higher-protein, lower-carbohydrate lifestyle that separates the Total Health Plan from other plans like the Zone, the South Beach Diet, and Atkins is that it's a more comprehensive and simpler way to gain control over your weight loss, wellness, and fitness goals.

The Total Health plan achieves this through promoting a positive mental attitude, exercise, and a healthy balance of quality protein choices and carbohydrates in the form of fiber-rich fruits and vegetables. It also offers an effective follow-up program for its readers by offering a *free* one-month subscription of customized weight loss and wellness menu options online at www.totalhealthdoc.com.

THE LOW-FAT DIET MYTH

The fact is, the classic low-fat, high-carbohydrate diet that we've been recommended to follow over the past twenty years *simply does not work!*

The American public is 32 percent fatter than twenty years ago. About

TOTAL HEALTH SUCCESS STORY

My Husband Says I Saved His Life

JACKIE P.
Contract manager

AGE: 56
HEIGHT: 5 FEET, 6 INCHES
TOTAL HEALTH START DATE: MAY 1999
START WEIGHT: 178 POUNDS
AFTER WEIGHT: 136 POUNDS
TOTAL WEIGHT LOSS: 42 POUNDS
START BODY FAT PERCENTAGE: 44%
AFTER BODY FAT PERCENTAGE: 29.5%
START FAT POUNDS: 78
AFTER FAT POUNDS: 38
TOTAL POUNDS OF FAT LOSS: 40

Jackie P. before

Jackie P. after

It's hard to believe that you can go through so much of your life with the wrong information. I've tried losing weight most of my life, and all these years I was eating the wrong stuff.

I didn't think it was possible to lose weight and feel good at the same time. Every diet left me feeling exhausted and lousy. Some of them helped me lose weight, but only while I bought their prepackaged diet meals. As soon as I went back to real-world food, it was a constant struggle not to regain the weight.

This program is different. For starters, I have a lot more energy, and I feel great! Total Health teaches you how to change your eating habits. It's not a diet, it's a way of eating, and you learn as you lose by eating the right kind of foods in the proper amounts. Everything you eat on this program, you can buy at the supermarket.

Total Health is very easy to follow. And I like having a coach who can answer questions and show me how to make the program work for me.

I've followed Dr. Markham's program for six months and lost 42 pounds.

People at work have told me how much more healthy I look. My skin looks better. I've also updated my wardrobe to go with my new body.

My husband is on the Total Health program, too. He was seeing an M.D. every three weeks to treat his high cholesterol and blood pressure. His doctor prescribed medication and a low—almost no—fat diet loaded with pasta. He lost a little weight, but his blood pressure and cholesterol didn't budge.

Then he started following the Total Health program. When he went for his regular checkup within three weeks, his doctor was astounded that his blood pressure and cholesterol levels were all down to normal. To date, my husband has lost 60 pounds. He's off his blood pressure medication and sees his M.D. only every six months for monitoring.

My husband tells me that I literally saved his life. And he looks great! I've been married thirty years, and it's like I have a new husband.

---

one out of three adults and one out of eight children is considered clinically obese. Obesity is defined as an excessive percentage of body fat which is considered unhealthy. An acceptable level of body fat in healthy women should range from 25 to 35 percent. A healthy range of body fat in men should be from 10 to 23 percent.

Obesity contributes to an estimated 300,000 deaths every year and is surpassing smoking as the leading cause of preventable of death. More than $100 billion is spent on obesity-related expenses in the United States each year, not including the $42.6 billion spent annually to shed excess weight. More than 53.6 million workdays are lost every year to obesity-related diseases, and American businesses are losing more than $4 billion per year in lost productivity.

Now, those are not very good statistics. The reason that the low-fat, high-carbohydrate diet does not work is simple: *fat does not make you fat!* That's right! Contrary to what nutritionists and the food industry have been spouting for decades, eating fat is not the reason so many Americans are overweight. The real culprit is the high carbohydrate content of our diets. I grew up in the state of Wisconsin, and we did not fatten the pigs and cows with fat, we fattened them with low-fat grain—the same foods the nutritional establishment has been telling us to eat for the past twenty years!

The way to understand why fat does not make you fat and low-fat grains do is to take a look at the dietary–hormonal connection and how food acts as a drug.

Food Is a Drug

The kind of food you eat has a tremendous effect on your body, your energy levels, your mental alertness, and the quality of your life. Like a drug, the food you eat causes powerful biochemical reactions in your body. The bottom line: the kind of food you eat and when you eat it tells your body whether to burn fat or store fat.

So how is food like a drug? First, like a drug, food can be very addictive. Second, like a drug, food causes strong biochemical reactions in your body. And finally, like a drug, food can be used or abused. We all know how easy it is to abuse food.

For some people, there are strong psychological forces behind their eating behavior. Some of these factors may relate to past or present emotional issues that can trigger unhealthy eating patterns, or what many people call "stress eating."

The first step in gaining control over our *emotions,* which cause *feelings* leading to potentially destructive eating patterns is protecting our *thoughts* related to the *events* in our daily lives. This is the basis of *cognitive behavioral therapy,* developed by Aaron Beck and used in the field of psychology to break destructive patterns.

Example

Let's say the *event* is that you're getting ready to go to work and discover that your husband has accidentally taken your only set of house keys and is already on a plane to Saint Louis for a business trip.

Your immediate *thought* is "Oh, my God, this is horrible! I'm going to be late for work, and my boss is going to fire me."

The *feelings* related to the emotions of your thoughts may be depression and anxiety about possibly losing your job.

The *action* or *behavior* associated with your feelings is to "stress eat" your way to the bottom of a box of Krispy Kreme donuts.

One of the keys to gaining control of your *actions* or *behavior* is to change your *thoughts,* which can change your *feelings.* So instead of the *thought* "That idiot husband of mine went off with my keys, and now I'm going to lose my job," leading to feelings of anger, depression, and anxiety, you may consider the *thought* "Well, I'll call the locksmith to make another key and catch up on some paperwork until it arrives." Thus you've changed your *thought* and avoided the negative *feelings* that could have resulted in a negative *action* or *behavior.*

Depending on the severity of past or present *events,* some of these issues may need to be worked out with professional help through appropriate counseling. But the good news is that the impulse to eat certain kinds of foods is not all in your head. When you get that craving for the M&M's in your bottom-right-hand desk drawer, there's some serious biochemistry at work, too.

The Hormonal Connection

Hormones are chemicals that are manufactured by special glands in your body and released into your bloodstream. Your blood transports hormones to different parts of your body, where they influence the way your organs and tissues work. Because hormones control and influence so many vital processes, such as growth, sexual drive, aging, and your metabolism, to name a few, hormone research is one of the most exciting fields of medical research.

Among the scientific findings to emerge from scientific studies is the strong connection between food and hormones. Specifically, the kind of food you eat and how much you eat triggers the release of two powerful hormones, insulin and glucagon.

What, you may ask, is so important about insulin and glucagon? The answer is simple: Insulin tells your body to *store* fat. Glucagon tells your body to *burn* fat. Therefore, we want to produce more fat-burning glucagon and less fat-storing insulin.

The Dangers of Excess Insulin

When you eat foods that produce too much insulin, such as bread and pasta, not only are you telling your body to store fat, but all that excess insulin boosts the production of triglycerides or blood fats. And what does blood fat do to your arteries? It clogs them, making you a prime candidate for a stroke or heart attack.

Excess insulin also stimulates the liver to produce cholesterol. This is why your cholesterol levels can still be high even if you cut all fats out of your diet. The amount of fat you eat does not influence your blood cholesterol levels much. The real culprit is excess insulin, which also contributes to high blood pressure.

I've saved the worst for last. When your body produces excess insulin on a regular basis, you are likely to develop insulin resistance. This is a vicious cycle in which the body becomes less sensitive to insulin and compensates by secreting more and more of the stuff.

The result: you store more and more fat and gain more and more weight. After a while, your pancreas, which produces insulin, cannot satisfy the demand. This is a precursor to developing a deadly disease called adult-onset diabetes.

Adult-onset diabetes, also known as type 2 diabetes, affects more than 8 million Americans. It is a devastating disease characterized by loss of energy and weight gain. People afflicted with diabetes suffer from blindness, heart disease, kidney failure, and circulatory problems that can lead to the amputation of fingers and toes. Diabetes is also a well-known cause of male impotence.

Scared? You should be. It's estimated that there are another 8 million Americans who suffer from some form of diabetes and don't even know it!

The Good News

Now take a deep breath. There is a proven way to get your body to reduce the amount of fat-storing insulin and promote the release of fat-burning glucagon. And you don't need expensive prescription medicines or prepackaged meals. The secret is to eat the right combination of everyday foods, in the right amounts, at the right times.

HOW TO COMBINE FOODS CORRECTLY

Whether your goal is to decrease your body fat, increase your energy, or get sick less often, the key to success starts with the proper combination of food. Your body has the complex task of managing a host of intricate functions to promote life and harmony. To do this, it needs fuel.

The body extracts fuel through a highly complex series of chemical reactions that begins with the digestion of food. Smaller compounds formed from the breakdown of food are then metabolized into the simple compounds water, carbon dioxide, and oxygen, which are easily disposed of by the body. This process of metabolism creates fuel for the body.

One simple analogy to your body's metabolism would be starting a fire in the fireplace. The log or wood would represent *food,* the heat of the fire would represent the *energy* produced, and the ash would represent the disposable *by-product*.

All food is composed of macronutrients (protein, carbohydrates, and fat), micronutrients (vitamins and minerals), and water. Apart from water, food is made up primarily of macronutrients. Macronutrients are the only food components that provide food energy, measured in calories, to maintain life.

Carbohydrates are various forms of simple sugars linked together in polymers (chains). Carbohydrates are found in the form of bread, pasta, rice, potatoes, fruits, juices, vegetables, and sweets. When you eat carbohydrate-rich foods, your body converts them into glucose, also known as blood sugar. The human body requires very little carbohydrate other than the amount needed for additional calories to provide energy and to nourish the tissues that require it: the red blood cells, parts of the eye, the kidneys, and the brain.

Protein comes in the form of beef, pork, and poultry; fish and seafood; soy protein, nuts, and dairy products such as eggs and cheese. Protein is made of amino acids, the building blocks that your body uses to make up your lean body mass (muscles), hair, skin, nails, and eyes. Nine of these amino acids, known as the *essential amino acids,* cannot be synthesized by your body and must be supplied by a high-quality protein.

Fat is found in high amounts in dairy products, such as butter, cheese, and eggs. We also see it on the edge of red meat, and it's found in nuts and oils. The important thing to know is that *fat does not make you fat!* In fact, you need the *right kind* of fat in your diet in the *right amount* to burn body fat and produce the hormones that are essential to good health.

The Hormonal Response to Food

The reason excess carbohydrate consumption leads to obesity has to do with your body's hormonal response to food.

When you eat a high-carbohydrate meal, such as pasta, French toast, or half a box of Ding Dongs, those carbs are rapidly converted into glucose, or blood sugar. As a result, your blood sugar level surges. At first, this makes your brain very happy. The brain is a glucose hog and consumes about two thirds of the glucose in your body for energy.

The spike in blood sugar also tells your pancreas to secrete insulin. Remember, the job of insulin is to reduce the amount of glucose in the bloodstream. It does this by storing excess glucose. First, a small amount is stored in your liver and muscles. The rest of the excess glucose is stored as body fat.

But it's not over yet. As I said, the brain craves glucose. And when insulin does its job of reducing excess glucose, there isn't enough glucose left for the brain to convert into energy. This is why you start to nod off after a big, carb-heavy meal.

So the brain sends a message: consume more carbohydrates! That's when you reach for your midmorning or midafternoon hit of M&M's. That's how you end up taking a ride on the blood sugar roller coaster, cycling dramatically from high to low energy. And that's how all those excess carbs become excess pounds. It's a vicious cycle that leads to obesity, insulin resistance, hypoglycemia, and worse.

> *The secret to breaking this cycle and taking control of your health is simple: Increase the amount of protein you eat and decrease the amount of carbohydrates.*

Eating the right amount of protein stimulates the release of glucagon, a hormone that helps stabilize your energy levels by mobilizing the release of the sugars stored in your liver to satisfy your brain's need for glucose (thus curbing and eventually ending your carbohydrate cravings). Another bonus: glucagon also helps your body burn stored body fat!

Instead of eating French toast for breakfast, have an omelet with fresh fruit. Rather than pasta for lunch, eat chicken, beef, fish, or your favorite protein entrée with vegetables. Now you won't be reaching for your midmorning or midafternoon hit of M&M's to satisfy your brain's cravings for sugar to increase your energy levels; you'll be burning stored fat and the stored sugars in your liver for energy rather than taking a ride on the "blood sugar roller coaster."

This is how food acts like a drug! There's not a drug company in the whole world, with unlimited financial resources and the top scientists, that could create a drug that could do a better job regulating your blood sugars, burning stored body fat, and increasing your energy level than the kind of food you eat, how much you eat, and when you eat it!

Don't get me wrong; I'm not saying all carbohydrates are bad for you. Carbohydrates are an essential part of healthy nutrition, as long as you eat the right amount and the right kind.

What makes one form of carbohydrate better than another? The answer is a carbohydrate's *glycemic index*—the rate at which a carbohydrate is converted into glucose, or sugar, in the bloodstream. *High-glycemic carbs* convert into sugar rapidly, causing an increased insulin response. *Low-glycemic carbs* convert into sugar at a slower rate, resulting in a reduced insulin response.

"Good" carbohydrates are *low glycemic.* "Bad" carbohydrates are *high glycemic.* If you want to live in Total Health, it is essential that you choose good carbohydrates over bad carbohydrates whenever possible.

One of the major determining factors of the glycemic index in fruits and vegetables is their content of natural fiber. The more natural fiber a fruit or vegetable contains, the lower its glycemic index. This is because fiber acts like a "brake," meaning that it takes the body longer to convert the fruit or vegetable carbohydrate source into sugar due to its natural fiber content.

Other nonfruit, nonvegetable sources of carbohydrates, such as bread, pasta, white rice, and potatoes, either are made with flour or are very starchy. This causes them to convert into sugar very rapidly. This rapid conversion into sugar, which causes a rapid rise in blood sugar levels, makes them very high glycemic.

So you want to choose low-glycemic, fiber-rich fruits and vegetables, such as apples, oranges, pineapple, broccoli, and cauliflower, as often as possible. You also want to limit your consumption of high-glycemic foods, such as bread, pasta, white rice, and potatoes. These foods are not entirely forbidden, but the less of them you eat, the better you'll feel. When consuming bread, pasta, and rice, choose whole grain types whenever possible. They're low glycemic and contain naturally higher amounts of fiber, vitamins, and minerals.

Note: See the complete Macronutrient Units list of low-glycemic carbohydrates on page 84 in the section "Eating Your Way to Total Health."

WHY FAT IS THE KEY TO GOOD HEALTH

Contrary to the nutritional "wisdom" most of us get from the media and food packaging, not all fat is bad for you. In fact, your body needs a certain amount of fat to nourish cells, supply essential fatty acids, and trigger the release of a hormone that signals your brain that you're full. Fat also slows down the conversion of carbohydrates into glucose, feeding your brain a steady flow of glucose, not a sudden rush that triggers an excess insulin response.

So why hasn't your doctor told you that fat is good? That it does not make you fat and isn't responsible for raising your cholesterol that much?

Unfortunately, your doctor, just like the general public, has been misinformed by studies (which many times are financed by the food industry). Also, medical schools spend very little time educating doctors on proper nutrition and disease prevention.

The fact that most medical doctors are not well informed about proper nutrition is really not their fault. The majority of their time in medical school is reserved for learning how to diagnose many different diseases and what types of medications or treatments to prescribe to combat those diseases. Therefore they must depend on the information they read in journals and publications outside of their normal education.

No medical doctor would disagree with the statement that proper diet and exercise are good for you. Unfortunately, much of the information they've been reading about proper diet is based on studies financed by the food industry. The food industry has made hundreds of millions and probably into the billions of dollars off the American public with this low-fat, nonfat diet craze.

How many people do you know who have had high cholesterol and were told by their physicians to cut out foods containing fat? How many people do you know who cut out fat and actually lowered their cholesterol levels? Probably not many.

Normally physicians are so busy diagnosing and treating their patients that they don't have the time to consult on proper nutrition. That's why they refer their patients to dieticians and nutritionists. In fact, about 30 to 40 percent of my patient referrals come from medical doctors.

Unfortunately, the majority of dieticians and nutritionists still believe the same misinformation about the high-carbohydrate, low-fat diet, much of which has been promoted by the present United States Department of Agriculture (USDA) Food Guide Pyramid.

Therefore their results with most patients are poor at best, and eventually the patients get frustrated and abandon all hope of gaining control of their health through diet and exercise.

Reevaluating the Food Guide Pyramid

The USDA Food Guide Pyramid has been taught in schools and seen in brochures and on food labels since 1992. It was originally developed to give Americans dietary guidelines to help them make better food choices.

Unfortunately, despite being a great graphic representation, the information on this pyramid doesn't reflect a healthy, balanced way of eating. That's because, as previously mentioned, it was based on flawed and biased scientific evidence. The shape of the pyramid is a great way to illustrate which foods should be eaten in higher quantities and which to consume more sparingly, but let's take a closer look at its present recommendations to reveal its flaws.

- **Bread, Cereal, Rice & Pasta Group (6–11 servings):** High-glycemic carbohydrates, such as bread, cereal, rice, and pasta, should never be considered a fundamental part of our diets. The USDA's recommendation of six to eleven servings per day borders on the dangerous, and the original reason for placing them in the base of the pyramid was to fill people up. This was meant to keep us from eating too much fat. Unfortunately, the message when the food pyramid was created in 1992 was that fat was the culprit in causing overweight and disease. This recommendation has almost single-handedly led to our present obesity epidemic. Remember: these types of carbohydrates convert into sugar and are stored as

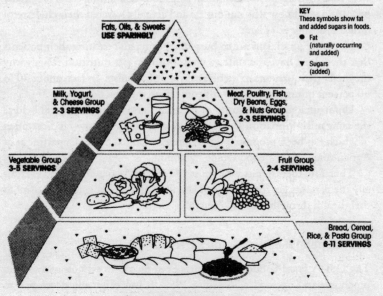

USDA Food Guide Pyramid

fat—the same way pigs and cows are fattened! High-glycemic carbohydrates in the form of bread, cereal, rice, and pasta should be used sparingly and replaced with carbohydrates in the form of fiber-rich fruits and vegetables.

- **Vegetables Group (3–5 servings) and Fruit Group (2–4 servings):** A diet rich in low-glycemic carbohydrates in the form of fiber-rich fruits and vegetables is a healthy one. The USDA's two to four servings of fruits and three to five servings of vegetables per day should remain the same.

- **Meat, Poultry, Fish, Dry Beans, Eggs & Nuts Group (2–3 servings):** Excluding dry beans, this is considered the protein group. Also, *all proteins are not created equal.* Leaner or low-fat sources of protein are better than higher-fat choices, but the USDA Food Guide Pyramid doesn't differentiate between naturally low-fat chicken and higher-fat sausage. The daily protein recommendations should be increased to five servings (at three meals and two snacks) per day, if you're choosing dairy options as a protein choice. The Milk, Yogurt & Cheese Group should also be incorporated into the protein group to avoid confusion.

- **Milk, Yogurt & Cheese Group (2–3 servings):** The calcium that dairy products supply is an essential component of healthy bones. The USDA's suggestions of two to three servings per day seems adequate, but this group needs to be incorporated into the protein category.

- **Fats, Oils & Sweets (use sparingly):** The USDA's recommendation of limiting saturated fats in the diet was good but needs to be updated to promote good fats in the form of essential fatty acids, and encourage avoidance of hydrogenated oils containing trans-fatty acids, such as margarine, as discussed later in this section. The good fats or essential fatty acids found in nuts and oils (olive oil, peanut oil, etc.) should be increased to three to five servings per day, with sweets remaining in the top of the pyramid to be used sparingly.

By the way, the USDA is not to blame. Its intention of promoting good health through the Food Guide Pyramid was pure. It was just misinformed, along with the rest of us. Now that the truth is out, discussions are already under way among officials to *turn the food pyramid upside down.*

On September 10, 2003, the USDA sent out a press release calling for public comments on technical support data for the Food Guide Pyramid. It also asked for public comments on proposed revisions to the daily food intake patterns that serve as the technical basis of the Food Guide Pyramid.

The USDA is reassessing the Food Guide Pyramid to ensure that it continues to be based on the most current, sound, and comprehensive science to help Americans make better food choices. The update of the pyramid is being coordinated with the 2005 Dietary Guidelines Advisory Committee as it reviews the Dietary Guidelines for Americans and recommends revisions to the USDA and the Department of Health and Human Services.

The Food Guide Pyramid reassessment and updating process has three phases:

1. Gathering information through technical research, professional and public input, and consumer research
2. Updating of the pyramid's daily food intake patterns to meet current nutritional standards
3. Developing new graphic and educational materials that will communicate pyramid messages in ways that consumers can more easily understand and put into practice

Many nutrition scientists who have criticized the content of the USDA's Food Guide Pyramid in the past are now proposing numerous alternatives, including Harvard's Healthy Eating Pyramid, the California Cuisine Food Pyramid, the Mediterranean Diet Pyramid, the Mayo Clinic Healthy Weight Pyramid, and others.

The final release of the updated Food Guide Pyramid and related consumer materials is scheduled for early 2005. For more information on the latest Food Guide Pyramid updates, visit the USDA's Web site at www.cnpp.usda.gov.

Eicosanoids: The Key to Wellness

Eating the *right kind* of fat is the key to boosting your immune system and staying healthy. That's because certain fats provide linoleic acid, the raw material that your body needs to produce amazing microhormones called *eicosanoids* (pronounced i-*co*-seh-noids).

The body of knowledge about eicosanoids is a relatively new, exciting, and ever-expanding area of scientific research. Think of eicosanoids as mas-

"Good" (Series One) Eicosanoids	"Bad" (Series Two) Eicosanoids
Enhance immunity	Suppress immunity
Decrease inflammation	Increase inflammation
Decrease pain	Increase pain
Increase oxygen flow	Decrease oxygen flow
Increase endurance	Decrease endurance
Prevent blood clotting	Promote blood clotting
Dilate airways	Constrict airways
Increase the rate of cell growth	Decrease the rate of cell growth

Note: Once again, "bad" is a relative term. For example, while "bad" eicosanoids may constrict blood vessels and airways, they also promote blood clotting, which keeps you from bleeding to death from a paper cut.

ter control hormones that regulate many of your body's biological functions, including the production of other hormones such as insulin and glucagon.

Your body manufactures two different families of eicosanoids: "good" eicosanoids (known as series one) and "bad" eicosanoids (series two).

Researchers continue to explore the link between the kinds of eicosanoids the body manufactures and wellness. Evidence continues to mount that poor health and disease may be due to your body making more "bad" eicosanoids than "good" ones. In other words, the key to good health is to promote the production of more good eicosanoids than bad ones.

Three Ways to Improve Your Eicosanoid Balance

1. Eat protein-rich, favorable-carbohydrate meals. As you know, following the Total Health eating program stimulates the release of fat-burning glucagon and inhibits the release of fat-storing insulin. These same powerful hormones also affect the production of good and bad eicosanoids. Insulin activates delta-5 desaturase, an enzyme that promotes the production of bad eicosanoids. Glucagon, which works in opposition to insulin, inhibits this enzyme.

Excess carbohydrates also inhibit another important enzyme called delta-6 desaturase. Delta-6 desaturase allows linoleic acid—the raw material your body needs to make all eicosanoids—to enter the eicosanoid production pathway. When this enzyme is blocked by too many carbohydrates, your body does not process all the linoleic acid it needs to produce eicosanoids.

Eating more protein and less carbohydrates is the most important step you can take to restore your eicosanoid balance.

2. Eat foods that supply plenty of linoleic acid. Linoleic acid is the essential fatty acid that your body uses as building blocks for all eicosanoids. Increasing the amount of linoleic acid in your body will give your body the supplies to produce eicosanoids. The best sources of linoleic acid are olive, almond, hazelnut, safflower, light sesame, sunflower, and walnut oils.

3. Stay away from trans-fatty acids. Trans-fatty acids are found in oils that have been altered by food manufacturers. Trans-fatty acids inhibit the delta-6 desaturase enzyme and the production of good eicosanoids. They have also been linked to heart disease.

One of the most common sources of trans-fatty acids is partially hydrogenated vegetable oil, the key ingredient in margarine, processed peanut butter, and thousands of other products. So look for natural peanut butter (the kind with the oil on the top), and go back to putting butter on your vegetables.

Don't mistake my recommendation to use butter as a license to go wild. We still want to use high-fat foods sparingly.

More Ways to Make Good Eicosanoids

For most people, eating protein-rich, favorable-carbohydrate meals, as well as fats rich in linoleic acid, and avoiding foods loaded with trans-fatty acids is enough to kick the production of good eicosanoids into high gear. But to tip the odds even more in your favor, here are three more ways to fine-tune your balance of eicosanoids:

1. Avoid foods with high levels of alpha-linoleic acid (ALA). ALA is another fatty acid that suppresses good eicosanoid production by inhibiting the delta-6 desaturase enzyme. ALA is found primarily in flaxseed oil, soybean oil, and canola oil. Instead, use olive oil, which has no ALA. If the distinctive taste of olive oil is a problem, another good choice is light sesame oil.

2. Watch your intake of arachidonic acid (AA). This fatty acid is found in the fat of red meat, organ meats, and egg yolks. Your body converts AA directly into bad eicosanoids. If you eat red meat, trim off the fat to avoid its high AA content. Instead of egg yolks, use egg whites or egg substitutes.

Watching the amount of arachidonic acid you ingest is important only if you are overly sensitive to large amounts. Signs of AA sensitivity include brittle hair and nails; dry, flaking skin; and minor rashes. If you are reducing excess insulin and producing more glucagon and are not experiencing these symptoms, you probably don't have a problem with AA.

3. Eat foods rich in eicosapentanoic acid (EPA). EPA is an essential fatty acid found in fish oil that slows the production of bad eicosanoids. Good sources of EPA include salmon, tuna, herring, and fish oil capsules.

HEART HEALTH

Understanding Your Blood Test/the Coronary Heart Disease Risk Ratio

Earlier we discussed the fact that fat is not the major culprit in clogging your arteries, leading to heart disease. Although we don't want to disregard the fat content of our food choices, the main cause of excess blood fats is eating too many high-glycemic carbohydrates, such as bread, pasta, rice, and potatoes.

These types of carbohydrates cause a rapid rise in blood sugars, creating an increased insulin response that many times leads to hyperinsulemia (too much insulin). Too much insulin in the blood causes our liver cells to produce excess cholesterol.

Many studies on fat have been financed by the food industry. Unfortunately this can lead to special interests on the part of the companies financing the studies, potentially creating a bias in regard to the results they hope to achieve.

Most studies over the years have used two groups of people—one group who ate a high-fat diet and another who ate a low-fat diet. The high-fat diet group had higher cholesterol levels, but both groups had about the same risk of potential heart disease.

The question you're probably asking is "why?" The answer lies in looking at the whole picture and what to look for in a blood test. We've been taught to focus mainly on our total cholesterol level, but actually the most important factor is our *coronary heart disease (CHD) risk ratio.*

To better demonstrate what we're talking about, let's take a look at a few terms and definitions associated with blood fats on a standard lipid profile blood test.

- *Cholesterol* is a fatlike substance made in the liver and found in the blood, brain, liver, and bile. It is essential to the production of sex hormones and can also be found in animal-source foods. The normal total cholesterol level should be less than 200 mg/dl.
- *LDL cholesterol* is low-density-lipoprotein cholesterol. It provides cholesterol for necessary body functions, but in excessive amounts it tends to accumulate in artery walls. That's why it's called "bad" cholesterol. The normal LDL cholesterol level is less than 160 mg/dl.
- *HDL cholesterol* is high-density-lipoprotein cholesterol. It's a type of cholesterol thought to help guard against atherosclerosis (clogged arteries). That's why it's called "good" cholesterol. The normal HDL cholesterol level is 50 mg/dl or higher.
- *Triglycerides* are combinations of glycerol with three of five different fatty acids. A large portion of the fatty substances (lipids) in the blood are triglycerides. The normal triglyceride level is less than 150 mg/dl.
- *The coronary heart disease (CHD) risk ratio* is the true determining factor of whether or not you're predisposed to coronary heart disease and a future heart attack. Many times your cholesterol can be elevated, but if your LDL (bad) cholesterol to HDL (good) cholesterol ratio is low, you're fine. When your HDL cholesterol is higher, it will offset the ill effects of a slightly elevated "bad" LDL cholesterol

level. A below-average risk ratio is between 2.7 and 4.0 in males and between 2.5 and 3.7 in females.

Remember, it's not the fat you eat that raises your cholesterol, blood pressure, or blood sugar level; it's the excess insulin from all those carbohydrates you've been eating.

Now that you know what to look for on a blood test, let's take a look at some actual "before and after" blood tests from one of my patients.

Case Study

Richard was a 44-year-old research scientist who was referred to me by the occupational health nurse at a local biotechnology company. He first went to the health nurse with complaints of fatigue, shortness of breath, and a general feeling of ill health. The nurse had been monitoring his progress through blood tests from his local M.D. and was concerned that despite his cutting out the fat from his diet and increasing his exercise, his weight loss and blood test results were still poor.

He had two children and a loving wife, but his high level of work-related stress and elevated blood fats were becoming a growing concern to his wife. She didn't want to become a widow raising two children without their father.

Like many of us, Richard was also caught up in a damaging pattern of skipping meals and not exercising regularly due to long workdays. By the time he arrived home from work, he was exhausted and starving. He would then overeat and after dinner would fall asleep in his favorite easy chair watching TV. The next day he would get up, go to work, and repeat the damaging cycle all over again—day after day, week after week, year after year.

The following is a copy of blood test results that he brought from his M.D. for my review. It showed a triglyceride level of 361 mg/dl, almost twice the high end of normal, which is between 50 and 190 mg/dl. His cholesterol was elevated at 268 mg/dl. Normal is between 130 and 200 mg/dl.

Blood Test 1: Before Total Health

Obviously, his physician was quite alarmed, so he ran a blood test a couple of months later and found that his cholesterol level had risen to 289 mg/dl and his triglyceride level was up to 561 mg/dl. His HDL level was 32 mg/dl, and his cholesterol-to-high-density-lipid risk ratio was at 9.0. That's well into the elevated coronary heart disease risk category. In other words, he was a heart attack waiting to happen. And he was just 44 years old!

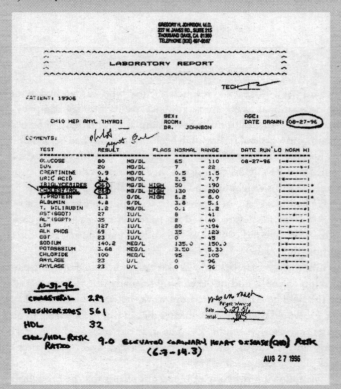

Blood Test 2: After Total Health

After seven weeks on the Total Health program, Richard's energy level increased and he dropped 30 pounds. His cholesterol level went from

289 mg/dl to 174 mg/dl, which is within the normal range. His triglyceride level dropped from 561 mg/dl to 107 mg/dl, which is smack in the middle of normal. His CHD risk ratio went from 9.0 to 3.7, which is below-average risk.

This was with no medications! This is not an extraordinary case, I have many pre and post blood tests of patients showing equal or even better results.

Richard was very happy, his M.D. was happy, his company nurse was happy, and, most important, his loving wife and children were the happiest.

Results like this in my private practice are great and very rewarding, but to continue to gain support for a more balanced approach to a low-carbohydrate lifestyle, more unbiased, government-based, non-food-industry-financed studies conducted by accredited institutions are needed.

A recent press release, issued on May 17, 2004, by the American Heart Association entitled "*Annals of Internal Medicine:* Low-Fat vs. Low-Carbohydrate Dietary Patterns for Weight Loss," appears to be the most balanced and sensible assessment to date. It states:

> Two randomized trials of low-fat versus low-carbohydrate weight loss diets, published in the May 18 issue of the *Annals of Internal Medicine,* found greater weight loss among the low-carbohydrate dieters at six months. One study ended at six months; however, the other study continued for twelve months, and found no difference in the amount of weight lost. Both studies found a greater reduction in triglycerides and a modest difference in high-density lipoprotein (HDL, the "good cholesterol") among the low-carbohydrate dieters. High levels of triglycerides, a type of blood fat, may be linked to an increased risk of coronary heart disease. In addition, both studies were small and had a high dropout rate of study participants, under-scoring both the difficulty in performing diet trials and of maintaining a weight-loss program that is based solely on diet.

The article goes on to quote Robert H. Eckel, chairman of the AHA Council on Nutrition, Physical Activity, and Metabolism, and professor of medicine at the University of Colorado Health Sciences Center:

> "Individuals who are trying to lose weight should consume a dietary pattern that has abundant scientific evidence behind it. A reduced-calorie diet rich in fruits, vegetables and whole grains, restricted in saturated fat and cholesterol, can help individuals lose weight and lower their risk of cardiovascular disease. It is important to get at least 30 and preferably 60 minutes of aerobic activity, such as brisk walking, daily. It's the long haul that really matters."

Choosing low-fat protein sources and not disregarding portion control or caloric intake as outlined in the Total Health plan will most likely be perceived by most health care professionals as a more balanced approach to long-term health when following a low-carbohydrate lifestyle.

TOTAL HEALTH SUCCESS STORY

I Was a Heart Attack Waiting to Happen

GREG B.
Insurance agent

Greg B. before

AGE: 53
HEIGHT: 6 FEET, 1 INCH
TOTAL HEALTH START DATE: OCTOBER 1999
START WEIGHT: 282 POUNDS
AFTER WEIGHT: 182 POUNDS
TOTAL WEIGHT LOSS: 100 POUNDS
START BODY FAT PERCENTAGE: 35%
AFTER BODY FAT PERCENTAGE: 17.4%
START FAT POUNDS: 99
AFTER FAT POUNDS: 32
TOTAL POUNDS OF FAT LOSS: 67
START LDL (BAD) CHOLESTEROL: 154 MG/DL
AFTER LDL (BAD) CHOLESTEROL: 111 MG/DL
START HDL (GOOD) CHOLESTEROL: 38 MG/DL
AFTER HDL (GOOD) CHOLESTEROL: 63 MG/DL
START TRIGLYCERIDES: 109 MG/DL
AFTER TRIGLYCERIDES: 56 MG/DL
START CHOLESTEROL: 214 MG/DL
AFTER CHOLESTEROL: 176 MG/DL
START CHOLESTEROL/HDL CORONARY RISK RATIO: 6.5
AFTER CHOLESTEROL/HDL CORONARY RISK RATIO: 1.9
START GLUCOSE (BLOOD SUGAR): 105 MG/DL
AFTER GLUCOSE (BLOOD SUGAR): 89 MG/DL
START WAIST MEASUREMENT: 52 INCHES
AFTER WAIST MEASUREMENT: 36 INCHES

Greg B. after

On Sunday, October 10, 1999, a good friend of mine told me about a young doctor who had helped him lose 10 pounds of excess weight, and it had been simple. So on Monday, October 11, 1999, I attended Dr. Markham's lecture to find out for myself if it was as simple as my friend had told me. His lecture was extremely informative, and the best thing about it was that it made sense!

On Tuesday, October 12, 1999, I was able to secure an appointment with Dr. Markham at 8:30 P.M. (Wow—a doctor who works late, how interesting!) He explained in detail what was expected of me, and he gave me a printout of my personalized Daily Menu that gave many options (including fast foods) for all the meal and snack times.

I weighed in at a whopping 282 pounds, my waist size was 52 inches, my neck size was 22 inches, my cholesterol was at 214 mg/dl, and my risk ratio was 6.5! Needless to say, I was a heart attack waiting to happen, not to mention the possibility of a stroke, and I was on my way to type 2 diabetes, if I didn't do something about it.

After approximately 18 months, I had lost 100 pounds, my waist size was 36 inches, my neck size was 16 inches, my cholesterol was 176 mg/dl, and my risk ratio was 1.9! I can now purchase all my clothes at regular clothing stores, not just big and tall shops. What a fantastic feeling—you have no idea!

Well, to say that it was simple is an understatement; it really *was* quite easy. Actually, the hardest thing for me to do was to remember to eat! Sounds strange, doesn't it? For me—and it's the same for everyone—it's a lifestyle change, not a diet. Why? Because when you go "on" a diet, the only other thing you can do is go "off" the diet! So you gain back all the weight you lost and more as a result.

Eating the way Dr. Markham suggests, three meals and two snacks at the appropriate times throughout the day, really works! I'm living proof of it! You have to imagine you're in charge of keeping the campfire going. By placing a few small pieces of wood on the fire, spaced apart appropriately, you'll be successful. However, if you throw a couple of large logs on the fire, you'll snuff it out.

That's how a correct daily eating habit works versus eating the wrong way. If you do it right, your body will burn fat and you'll lose weight slowly (6 to 8 pounds per month), but if you eat incorrectly or not at all, your body will convert to "storage or conserve mode" and you won't burn fat!

I also used Dr. Markham as my weekly accountability partner. His encouragement and sometimes scolding, if I didn't do something right, was a major factor in my success!

Bottom line: I owe my life to Dr. Markham and his Total Health concept. If you don't believe me, just ask my wife and children. Thanks again, Dr. Doug!

Your patient, but most important now, your friend,

Greg B.

TOTAL HEALTH SUCCESS STORY

I Was Able to Reduce My Diabetes Medications

GEORGE P.
Retired

George P. before

AGE: 73
HEIGHT: 5 FEET, 10 INCHES
TOTAL HEALTH START DATE: FEBRUARY 2000
START WEIGHT: 254 POUNDS
AFTER WEIGHT: 197 POUNDS
TOTAL WEIGHT LOSS: 57 POUNDS
START BODY FAT PERCENTAGE: 36.8%
AFTER BODY FAT PERCENTAGE: 27.1%
START FAT POUNDS: 93
AFTER FAT POUNDS: 53.5
TOTAL POUNDS OF FAT LOSS: 39
START LDL (BAD) CHOLESTEROL: 77 MG/DL
AFTER LDL (BAD) CHOLESTEROL: 75 MG/DL
START HDL (GOOD) CHOLESTEROL: 45 MG/DL
AFTER HDL (GOOD) CHOLESTEROL: 37 MG/DL
START TRIGLYCERIDES: 218 MG/DL
AFTER TRIGLYCERIDES: 85 MG/DL
START CHOLESTEROL: 166 MG/DL
AFTER CHOLESTEROL: 129 MG/DL
START CHOLESTEROL/HDL CORONARY RISK RATIO: 3.7
AFTER CHOLESTEROL/HDL CORONARY RISK RATIO: 3.5
START GLUCOSE (BLOOD SUGAR): 224 MG/DL
AFTER GLUCOSE (BLOOD SUGAR): 114 MG/DL
START WAIST MEASUREMENT: 44 INCHES
AFTER WAIST MEASUREMENT: 36 INCHES

George P. after

I first met Dr. Markham on February 8, 2000, when I was referred to him by my medical doctor. My blood fats were elevated, and my blood sugar was out of control, even with the use of several blood sugar–lowering medications. If I didn't lose the weight and get my blood sugar in balance through dietary changes, my doctor was going to start me on insulin injections.

My wife was already monitoring my diet and working hard to prepare low-fat meals. We would have pasta with low-fat red sauce, and I stayed away from fats completely. We thought we were doing all the right things, but we still couldn't get my weight under control.

When my wife and I first consulted with Dr. Markham, we were shocked when we found out we were doing all the wrong things! The very-low-fat choices we were making were actually raising my blood sugar and contributing to my weight gain.

Even though Dr. Markham was supportive of making low-fat choices, he explained that the high-glycemic types of carbohydrates, such as pasta, were converting into sugar rapidly and ending up being stored in my fat, just like in the pigs and cows in his home state of Wisconsin.

My wife and I got a kick out of his "corny"—no pun intended—midwestern sense of humor. His simple explanation, which is also outlined in his book, made perfect sense to my wife and me. So my wife started preparing foods recommended in Dr. Doug's Total Health plan. Within weeks the weight started to drop off.

The most dramatic thing was that my blood sugar started to test lower and lower by the day. Within several months of starting Dr. Doug's Total Health plan, my medical doctor was able to take me off two of three of my medications! My wife, my doctor, and I were thrilled by these remarkable results!

Oh, by the way, my wife, who was also overweight, went on to lose over 40 pounds just by eating the same way I did. This was great because she needed a knee replacement but her orthopedic doctor wouldn't do the surgery until she lost weight.

Now that she's had the surgery and I've lost weight, we're enjoying a happy and healthy retirement, thanks to Dr. Doug's Total Health plan.

For more information on heart disease and stroke, visit the American Heart Association's Web site, www.americanheart.org.

How to Reduce the Amount of Medications You Take

Caution: Never reduce or discontinue prescription medications without the consent and direction of your physician!

The key to potentially reducing or discontinuing prescription medications and the use of medications related to high blood pressure, high cholesterol, and adult-onset diabetes is blood sugar regulation.

Whether you're suffering from excess weight gain leading to high blood pressure or a high cholesterol level as a result of your own liver cells' production of excess cholesterol, or your cells are developing a resistance to insulin, the culprit is excess carbohydrate consumption leading to elevated blood sugars.

Once you start following the Total Health protein-rich, favorable-carbohydrate way of eating, you'll start to realize the benefits of controlled blood sugars. Your excess weight will start coming off, your sustained energy level will start to increase, your cholesterol will begin to decline, your blood pressure will start to decline, and your blood sugar level will drop.

Therefore, if you're taking medications to lower your cholesterol level or your blood pressure, or if you're taking medications for the beginning stages of adult-onset diabetes, you should be able to go back to your doctor to start monitoring your progress and begin lowering your medications.

In many cases, as with many of my own patients, your doctor will be able to completely eliminate your medications for high blood pressure, high cholesterol, and adult-onset diabetes.

Note: If you're taking blood sugar medications, it's very important that you monitor your blood sugar level on a daily basis. This is because as your blood sugar level starts to lower naturally, the blood sugar–lowering medications will drive it down even further.

Low blood sugar, also known as hypoglycemia or insulin reaction, can be defined as a blood glucose level below 60 to 70 mg/dl. It's usually accompanied by one or more symptoms, which may include shaking, sweating, irritability, headache, tingling, hunger, blurred vision, dizziness and confusion, numbness of the lips, nausea or vomiting, accelerated heart rate, sudden tiredness, seizures, pale appearance, frequent sighing, personality change, confusion, poor concentration, light-headedness, and loss of consciousness.

If you experience any of these symptoms or your blood sugar consistently tests low, *you must consult with your doctor immediately so he or she can start reducing your blood sugar–lowering medications. The same holds true for blood pressure medications.*

Always consult with your physician before making any kind of change in your diet or medications!

Part II

Following the Total Health Plan

OVERVIEW

The key to any weight loss and wellness program is accountability and proper follow-up. After several thousand in-office weight loss and wellness consultations, I have noted that the patients who achieve the best results are those who have committed to weekly follow-up visits.

When I first started writing *Total Health,* I struggled with how to offer my readers the same customized weight loss and wellness menu options that I give my patients. The other dilemma was offering the same kind of effective accountability and proper follow-up that my patients received on a weekly basis. The only answer was to write a book that would give people a simple way to understand why they should follow a protein-rich, favorable-carbohydrate way of eating and give them a more effective way to follow through properly with their weight loss and wellness goals.

I didn't want my book to be like all of the others, collecting dust up on a shelf because it was too technical or full of generic diets and menus that most people could not implement in their daily lives. Therefore I created www.totalhealthdoc.com to help people take control of their health, using the same proven principles and customized menus that have helped thousands of my own patients. On the Web site you can find:

- Menus and food choices customized for your body size, weight loss, and health goals
- Easy-to-follow food options for breakfast, lunch, dinner, and snacks that make it easy to know what to eat and when
- An extensive list of everyday protein-rich, favorable-carbohydrate foods that offers variety and flexibility
- More than 120 protein-rich, favorable-carbohydrate recipes

- Food preparation tips for dining out in Total Health
- Convenient fast-food options for drive-through dining
- Total Health success tips to speed your progress
- Personalized weight loss and wellness guidance via e-mail

Dieters who received personalized weight loss guidance via e-mail shed more pounds than those who didn't get extra help, according to an updated study by researchers at the Brown University School of Medicine in Providence, Rhode Island. Visit www.totalhealthdoc.com for personalized weight loss and wellness guidance.

Total Health Success Tips

• **Weigh yourself once a week.** This is necessary to monitor your progress on your Total Health program. Some people choose to weigh themselves daily. Also, there may be times when your body is redistributing its muscle and fat percentages. This means that you may gain 2 pounds of muscle (which is good) and lose 2 pounds of fat. The scale weight won't reflect weight loss, but your body fat percentage will have gone down due to the 2 pounds of fat loss. This translates into inches lost!

• **Choose healthy carbohydrates** in the form of fiber-rich fruits and vegetables with a low glycemic index. These are listed on the Macronutrient Units list (page 84). Strictly limit your consumption of pasta, rice, bread, and grains.

• **Choose healthy fat sources,** such as olive oil and nut oils. You will also maintain a low-fat diet naturally by eating lean meat, poultry, seafood, and low-fat dairy and vegetarian protein products.

• **Drink plenty of water,** up to eight glasses a day. You may also choose any sugar-free beverage such as diet sodas, Crystal Light beverages, etc. Hot tea, iced tea, and coffee are allowed. Use sugar substitutes to sweeten. If using an artificial sweetener such as aspartame is unappealing, try Splenda, which is made from sucralose. Stevia, a natural sweetener, is also available at health stores. See the "Sweeteners" section (page 59) for more details on sugar substitutes.

I also suggest the use of sugar-free syrups for coffee, plain yogurts, etc. There are now many great-tasting sugar-free flavors such as chocolate, hazelnut, caramel, vanilla, and others.

Refer to Appendix B, "Recommended Products," for sugar-free syrups.

TOTAL HEALTH SUCCESS STORY

I Lost Weight Even Without a Thyroid

SUE M.
Accounting clerk

Age: 63
Height: 5 feet, 7 inches
Total Health start date: October 1999
Start weight: 206 pounds
After weight: 154 pounds

Sue M. before

Total weight loss: 52 pounds
Start body fat percentage: 42%
After body fat percentage: 32.4%
Start fat pounds: 86
After fat pounds: 50
Total pounds of fat loss: 36
Start LDL (bad) cholesterol: 145 mg/dl
After LDL (bad) cholesterol: 118 mg/dl
Start HDL (good) cholesterol: 66 mg/dl
After HDL (good) cholesterol: 66 mg/dl
Start triglycerides: 162 mg/dl
After triglycerides: 92 mg/dl
Start cholesterol: 243 mg/dl

After cholesterol: 202 mg/dl

Sue M. after

Start cholesterol/HDL coronary risk ratio: 3.7
After cholesterol/HDL coronary risk ratio: 3.1
Start blood pressure: 176/96
After blood pressure: 134/82

I met Dr. Markham five years ago. I enjoyed his presentation and thought I would give his Total Health plan a try. I figured that I would probably lose some weight, get bored, and quit. This was my pattern due to my numerous failed diet attempts, including WeightWatchers. Instead it became the best diet I'd ever done—mainly because the Total Health plan wasn't a diet but a healthy way of eating.

I also had my thyroid removed in 1989 and was told that it was going to be extra hard to lose weight. I was getting very frustrated because along with my weight, my cholesterol level and blood sugar were on the rise. In fact, my M.D. said that if I didn't start losing weight, he was going to have to put me on cholesterol-lowering medications, as well as blood sugar medications for the beginning stages of adult-onset diabetes.

I started the program in October 1999, and it took only about seven months for me to lose over 50 pounds. This exceeded my goal of losing my weight by July 2000. My goal was to surprise my family on a return trip to my native country of Sweden for my sixtieth birthday celebration. My family in Sweden hardly recognized me when I got off the plane.

I feel great and very proud to say that I am keeping my weight down. My cholesterol went down, and I am no longer a borderline diabetic. If I can do this, anyone can. Even though I'm also a proud grandmother, it's nice to look too young to be a grandmother. If you don't believe me, just look at my before and after pictures!

Thank you, Dr. Markham!

- **A glass of wine or light beer is allowed,** but not by itself. Because these beverages contain up to 4 grams of carbohydrates, you must consume them with protein. Have your wine or beer with lunch or dinner or with some cheese as a snack. Mixed drinks are also acceptable as long as you use a sugar-free mixer. Example: vodka with sugar-free tonic.

Believe it or not, distilled alcohols, such as vodka, rum, whiskey, gin and so forth, have zero net carbohydrate value. Therefore, distilled alcohols are the preferred alcoholic beverages of choice.

- **Get enough fiber.** Adequate fiber intake is essential for healthy digestion. To make sure you get enough fiber, take over-the-counter fiber supplements or sugar-free orange-flavored Metamucil mixed into 8 to 10 ounces of drinking water. Drink up to 2 glasses a day.

Refer to "Appendix B, "Recommended Products," in the back of the book for recommendations of fiber supplements.

- **Take a high-quality vitamin and mineral supplement daily.**
- **Use the "ballpark" technique.** When dining out or when in doubt, this is an easy way to make sure you eat the proper amount of protein and carbohydrates. Keep your protein choice (meat, poultry, or fish) to a portion about the size of the palm of your hand—roughly 4 ounces. Choose a salad or vegetable portion about twice the size of your protein portion. Example: Caesar salad with grilled chicken. (Remember to take it easy on the croutons, and don't eat any bread.)

READING FOOD LABELS

One of the most confusing things for most consumers is understanding how to read a food label and how what's listed there relates to our health. Now, with the recent flood of new low-carb products onto the market to serve more than 59 million low-carb consumers, food labels have become even more confusing.

We will discuss how to read a "low-carb" label in a moment, but first we need to know the following information about the new food label provided by the U.S. Food and Drug Administration.

The New Food Label

Under regulations of the Food and Drug Administration of the Department of Health and Human Services and the Food Safety and Inspection Service of the U.S. Department of Agriculture, the food label offers more complete, useful, and accurate nutrition information than ever before.

The goal was to provide consumers with the following information:

- Nutrition information about almost every food in the grocery store
- Distinctive, easy-to-read formats that enable consumers to find the information they need to make healthful food choices more quickly
- Information on the amount per serving of saturated fat, cholesterol, dietary fiber, and other nutrients of major health concern
- Nutrient reference values, expressed as % Daily Values, that help consumers see how a food fits into an overall daily diet
- Uniform definitions for terms that describe a food's nutrient content—such as "light," "low fat," and "high fiber"—to ensure that such terms mean the same thing for any product on which they appear
- Claims about the relationship between a nutrient or food and a disease or health-related condition, such as calcium and osteoporosis, and fat and cancer; these are helpful for people who want to eat foods that may help keep them healthier longer
- Standardized serving sizes, which make nutritional comparisons of similar products easier
- Declaration of the total percentage of juice in juice drinks. This enables consumers to know exactly how much juice is in a product

Understanding the Food Label

To help you understand the food label, I will discuss the following food label graphic point by point.

Nutrition Facts

The first listing under "Nutrition Facts" is "Serving Size." The serving size is based on household and metric measures. The FDA defines household measures as cup, tablespoon, teaspoon, piece, slice, fraction (for example, ¼ pizza), and common household containers such as a jar or tray.

Metric measures are listed in grams (g) and milliliters (ml).

Amount Per Serving

This lists the total calories per serving as well as the calories from fat. This helps us keep track of our fat consumption and follow the recommendation of not obtaining more than 30% of our calories from fat.

% Daily Value

The % Daily Value shows the percentage of nutrients of the product per serving based on a 2,000-calorie-per-day diet. These nutrients refer to calories from total fat, saturated fat, cholesterol, sodium, total carbohydrate, dietary fiber, sugars, protein, vitamins A and C, calcium, and iron.

Calories per Gram

The calories per gram at the bottom of the food label shows the energy-producing macronutrients: fat, carbohydrate, and protein.

I feel the FDA did a great job in the concept and design of the new food label, which gives us the opportunity to know the fat, carbohydrate, and protein content of our food and to maintain the appropriate ratios when following the Total Health plan.

For more information on the specific details and updates to food labeling, contact:

Nutrition Facts

Serving Size ½ cup (114g)
Servings Per Container 4

Amount Per Serving

Calories 90   Calories from Fat 30

	% Daily Value*
Total Fat 3g	5%
Saturated Fat 0g	0%
Cholesterol 0mg	0%
Sodium 300mg	13%
Total Carbohydrate 13g	4%
Dietary Fiber 3g	12%
Sugars 3g	
Protein 3g	

Vitamin A 80%	•	Vitamin C 60%
Calcium 4%	•	Iron 4%

* Percent Daily Values are based on a 2,000 calorie diet. Your daily values may be higher or lower depending on your calorie needs.

	Calories:	2,000	2,500
Total Fat	Less than	65g	80g
Sat Fat	Less than	20g	25g
Cholesterol	Less than	300mg	300mg
Sodium	Less than	2,400mg	2,400mg
Total Carbohydrate		300g	375g
Dietary Fiber		25g	30g

Calories per gram:
Fat 9 • Carbohydrate 4 • Protein 4

New Food Label Guide

FDA

General Inquiries: Call toll-free (888) INFO-FDA (888) 463-6332).
Food Safety Hotline: (800) 332-4010
The FDA's food label information on the Web: www.cfsan.fda.gov/label.html.

Meat and Poultry Hotline: (800) 535-4555

For information on labeling in the UK, contact the Food Standards Agency:
FSA Hotline: 020 7276 8000
The FSA's food label information on the Web: www.food.gov.uk/foodlabelling
Meat Hygiene Service: 01904 455601

Understanding the Label on a "Low-Carbohydrate" Food

As you may be aware, there is considerable concern about and confusion as to the nutritional labeling of low-carbohydrate foods. Due to this confusion, the FDA is presently adopting new guidelines to inform and protect low-carb consumers.

Most of the confusion lies in the way carbohydrates are viewed and calculated. Food is divided into five main categories:

- Fat
- Protein
- Moisture
- Ash (minerals)
- Carbohydrates

The government calculates by *difference,* which means that anything that is not fat, protein, moisture, or ash is lumped into the carbohydrate category. This includes sugars and sugar alcohols. Carbohydrates can be further subdivided into:

- Sugars (sucrose, lactose, maltose, fructose, glucose)
- Fibers
- Sugar alcohols (maltitol, sorbitol, lactitol, isomalt, mannitol, xylitol, HSH [hydrogenated starch hydrolysate], and erythritol).

Low-carbohydrate food producers recognize the government's method of categorizing ingredients as carbohydrates, but we must also take into account the effects of the various ingredients on the body.

The food producers have designed a new label to meet the government's methods and requirements. Whereas they used to omit the sugar alcohols from the total carbohydrate count on the nutritional panel, they now include it. In addition to this change, they now include a "Carbohydrate Facts" panel (see below) to show you the *net effective carbohydrates.* These net effective carbohydrates include only those carbohydrates that have a notable effect on your blood sugar levels.

Fiber and sugar alcohols can be subtracted from the total carbohydrate count.

Example

Total carbohydrates	32 g
– Fiber	10 g
– Sugar alcohols	20 g
Net effective carbs	2 g

LOW-CARBOHYDRATE AND HIGH-PROTEIN PRODUCTS

In 1996, when I first began counseling patients on a more balanced approach to a low-carbohydrate lifestyle, low-carb products were few and far between. I would recommend eating sandwiches without the top piece of bread (open-faced), and wrapping burgers in lettuce instead of a bun. Two of the few free snack choices available at the time were sugar-free Jell-O and homemade sugar-free Popsicles made with diet soda or Crystal Light beverages.

In fact, I provided the fast-food industry with one of the first comprehensive plans for offering healthier, low-carb menu options. Now almost every fast-food chain in the country is jumping on the low-carb bandwagon. This is great, and due to the more than 59 million low-carb consumers, we now have hundreds of new low-carb products available in the marketplace.

The low-carb revolution is definitely upon us, and it's here to stay. After almost eight years of having very few low-carb options to recommend to my patients, it's exciting to see many food manufacturers creating great-tasting, high-quality, low-carb products, ranging from tasty chocolate bars and ice cream to breads, cereals, and sodas. Unfortunately, not all low-carb products and their ingredients are created equal. This also holds true for non-low-carb processed foods.

Despite the great news about increased product availability, it's still very important for low-carb consumers to scrutinize the labels of low-carb products for their ingredients, potential side effects, and overall health benefits. Even though I'm an advocate of quality low-carb products, I recommend choosing natural whole foods in the form of quality low-fat proteins and carbohydrates in the form of fiber-rich fruits and vegetables whenever possible.

Remember, low-carb products in the form of meal replacements and "zero net carb" snacks shouldn't be used to replace real foods. They should be used in moderation for when you're in a time crunch or need to curb that occasional sweet tooth.

You may want to consider the following points when choosing low-carb products:

• *What sugar substitutes are used to sweeten the low-carb product?* An in-depth description of sweeteners can be found in the "Sweeteners" section (page 59), but let's take a look at the potential side effects of a few.

Many low-carb candies and products are sweetened with sugar alcohols. Sugar alcohols are considered nutritive or caloric sweeteners. Even though they have zero net effective carbs, they still contain calories. Due to the slow absorption of many sugar alcohols, such as maltitol, they may cause abdominal cramping, gas, and diarrhea when consumed in excessive amounts. Therefore, low-carb products containing sugar alcohols should not be consumed in excessive amounts. The sugar alcohol called *erythritol,* due to its faster rate of absorption, is far less likely to cause undesirable side effects. It also contains fewer calories than most sugar alcohols and therefore is my favored choice of a sugar alcohol.

The only noncaloric sweetener made from real sugar is called *sucralose* and goes by the trade name Splenda. It contains no calories, zero effective carbs, no aftertaste, and no known side effects. Therefore Splenda is my sweetener of choice.

• *What's the fat content of the low-carb product?* Remember, fat contains calories and the breakdown of certain types of fats causes toxins and other potential long-term health risks such as cancer and heart disease.

• *Does the low-carb product contain hydrogenated oils?* The by-products of hydrogenated oils are trans-fatty acids. Trans–fatty acids have been linked to heart disease.

• *What types of preservatives, level of sodium content, and food additives does the low-carb product contain?* The same scrutiny used in reading conventional food labels in regard to sodium content should be exercised with low-carb labels, particularly for people with high blood pressure or potential allergies to artificial preservatives such as monosodium glutamate, food colorings, and so on. Let's not replace one set of problems with another.

Refer to APPENDIX B, "Recommended Products" for recommendations of high-quality, good-tasting, low-carb products.

MICRONUTRIENTS: VITAMINS AND MINERALS

If you're like most Americans, chances are you have at least one—and probably several—half-full bottles of vitamin and mineral supplements in your medicine cabinet.

And no wonder. It seems that every day some new study or article or health guru states that vitamin X or mineral Y will help you stay healthy or prevent some horrible disease. Then, the next day, a new study or article or guru says the stuff you just bought is no good. Worse, vitamin X can actually cause a different but equally horrible disease. What you really need is Vitamin Z!

Thanks to an increasingly health-conscious public and relentless marketing, sales of vitamins and other nutritional supplements have skyrocketed. According to the Council for Responsible Nutrition, a trade group for the supplement industry, an estimated 100 million Americans are spending $6.5 billion a year on vitamins, minerals, and nutritional supplements. That's up from $3 billion in 1990.

Two factors are driving the explosive growth in supplement sales. First, as the baby boomers get older, more and more people are becoming active participants in their own health care. This consumer health care movement is being fueled by easier access to medical information and acceptance by traditional medical organizations of health care options such as acupuncture and chiropractic.

The other reason for all the marketing hype about nutritional supplements is the Dietary Supplement Health and Education Act of 1994. This law allows supplement makers to market their products as "dietary supplements" and thus avoid the scientific scrutiny and expense of the FDA prescription drug review process. As long as supplement manufacturers do not claim that their products offer specific health benefits, they're free to sell their wares over the counter, through mail order, and over the Internet.

Confused?

The following pages will help you sort through the hype. We'll start with a brief review of vitamin and mineral fundamentals. Then we'll take a closer look at how vitamin and mineral supplements, water, and fiber contribute to optimal health.

Vitamin and Mineral Basics

Even though we can increase our energy levels, reduce our body fat, and increase our immunity against disease through the Total Health eating plan, our bodies also require *micronutrients* for ultimate performance.

Micronutrients—commonly known as vitamins and minerals—are essential to life. They perform a multitude of functions that involve the efficient use and disposal of the macronutrients (protein, carbohydrates, and fat). The body isn't able to produce micronutrients, and nowadays we're unable to get enough even with a proper diet.

This is due largely to environmental factors such as increased air pollution and decreased food nutrient value caused by the depleted mineral content of our soil. Therefore, we must choose the appropriate multivitamin/mineral supplement that will ensure we have the necessary amounts of these essential micronutrients for our body to manage the complex functions required for an active healthy lifestyle.

Before we can choose the right vitamin and mineral supplement, we must first learn about the terms and definitions associated with vitamins and minerals.

Vitamins

Vitamins are organic and allow your body to process carbohydrates, proteins, and fats. They also act as catalysts by triggering or speeding up chemical reactions. There is a total of thirteen vitamins, which nutritionists classify into two groups: *fat soluble* and *water soluble*.

The fat-soluble vitamins are A, D, E, and K. They're called fat-soluble because they're stored in your body's fat. They're usually found together in the fats and oils of food and require bile for absorption. Once absorbed, they're stored in the liver and fatty tissues until the body needs them. Any disease that prevents fat absorption, such as a liver disease that prevents bile production, can bring about deficiencies of the fat-soluble vitamins. Deficiencies are also likely when people eat diets that are extremely low in fat.

Vitamins A and D can act somewhat like hormones, directing cells to store and release or convert substances. Vitamin E circulates all over the body, preventing oxidative damage to tissues. This oxidative or cellular damage is explained further under "Antioxidants" (page 50).

The other nine vitamins are water soluble and aren't stored in large amounts in your body. The water-soluble vitamins include vitamin C and the eight B vitamins—thiamine (B_1), riboflavin (B_2), niacin (B_3), pyridoxine (B_6), pantothenic acid, cyanocobalamin (B_{12}), biotin, and folic acid (folate).

The body absorbs them easily and just as easily excretes them in the urine. The water-soluble vitamins help the body metabolize carbohydrates, lipids, and amino acids. The B vitamins are considered coenzymes, which are small molecules that combine with enzymes to make them active. The B vitamins work together with enzymes in the metabolism of energy and nutrients and the creation of new cells.

RECOMMENDED DIETARY ALLOWANCES (RDAS) FOR VITAMINS
IU (international units); mcg (micrograms)
(Ages 25–50 years unless otherwise noted)

VITAMIN A
3,330 IU (men)
2,664 IU (women)

BETA-CAROTENE
No RDA exists for beta-carotene

VITAMIN D
200 IU (ages 19–51)*
400 IU (ages 51–70)*
600 IU (age 70+)*

VITAMIN E
14.9 IU (men)
11.92 IU (women)

VITAMIN K
80 mcg (men)
65 mcg (women)

VITAMIN B COMPLEX:
Thiamine (B₁)
1.2 mg (men)
1.1 mg (women)

Riboflavin (B₂)
1.3 mg (men)
1.1 mg (women)

Niacin
16 mg (men)
14 mg (women)

Pyridoxine (B₆)
MEN:
1.3 mg (ages 19–50)
1.7 mg (ages 51+)

WOMEN:
1.3 mg (ages 19–50)
1.5 mg (ages 51+)

Folic acid
400 mcg

VITAMIN B₁₂
2.4 mcg

Biotin
30 mcg*

Pantothenic acid
5 mg*

VITAMIN C
60 mg

---

* Updated RDAs have not been set for vitamin D, biotin, and pantothenic acid.
  Recommendations for daily intake are based on a value known as "adequate intake."

Sources: *Dietary Reference Intakes: Calcium, Phosphorus, Magnesium, Vitamin D and Fluoride* (Washington, DC: National Academy Press, 1997); *Dietary Reference Intakes for Thiamin, Riboflavin, Niacin, Vitamin B₆, Folate, Vitamin B₁₂, Pantothenic Acid, Biotin and Choline* (Washington, DC: National Academy Press, 1998).

Minerals

Minerals are inorganic substances that promote a variety of important bio-chemical processes. There are fifteen dietary minerals, which nutritionists also classify into two groups: *major minerals* are needed in amounts greater than 100 milligrams a day; *trace minerals* are needed in amounts less than 100 milligrams a day.

The major minerals include calcium, phosphorus, magnesium, sodium, chloride, potassium, and sulfur. The trace minerals required for human health are iron, iodine, copper, manganese, zinc, boron, selenium, and chromium. These are used by the body to burn fat, build muscle, and strengthen bones as well as to promote healing and oxygen delivery to the cells.

How Much Do You Need?

When it comes to taking vitamin and mineral supplements, the question "how much?" is a source of continuing controversy.

Most established medical, scientific, and nutritional sources say you get all the vitamins and minerals you need from eating a balanced diet; follow the general nutritional guidelines, such as the Recommended Dietary Allowances (RDAs), and you'll be fine.

Good advice, but do you eat a balanced diet? Do you know anyone who does? That's the big problem with the notion that the food you eat provides all the vitamins and minerals you need. Most Americans don't eat the wide variety of foods necessary to obtain sufficient amounts of the micronutrients they need.

For example, in a study published in *The New England Journal of Medicine* in March 1998, researchers from the Harvard Medical School estimated that 40 percent of Americans may have a vitamin D deficiency. Forty percent!

Our rushed, junk-food, no-time-for-breakfast-or-lunch, prepackaged, processed, frozen-food culture does not encourage a balanced diet. And as you know, if you're not eating the right balance of foods in the right amount, vitamin and mineral deficiencies may be the least of your problems! No multivitamin supplement will compensate for lousy eating habits.

Are the RDAs High Enough?

Since 1941, the Food and Nutrition Board of the Institute of Medicine, National Academy of Sciences, has set RDAs for the minimum amount of vitamins and minerals needed to prevent diseases caused by vitamin and mineral deficiencies.

For years, this approach has been criticized by a growing and increasingly vocal number of respected medical researchers and doctors. They argue that the intake levels dictated by the RDAs are just enough to help you survive, not thrive. Instead, vitamins and minerals should be taken in amounts that prevent chronic diseases and promote optimal health, a state in which your body functions at its best.

It's taken some time, but the government nutrition experts, the folks who set the official nutritional standards, are catching up. Slowly but surely, RDAs are being reset to recommend higher amounts of specific vitamins and minerals.

In 1997, the board announced that the RDAs were now just one part of an expanded set of nutritional guidelines called Dietary Reference Intakes (DRIs). The DRIs reflect the latest scientific consensus on the role vitamins and minerals play in optimum health. For example, the first DRI report, on calcium, revised intake levels upward to prevent bone loss caused by osteoporosis instead of just preventing calcium deficiency.

New DRIs for folate and other B vitamins were published in 1998. As funding becomes available, new DRIs—which will include updated and expanded RDAs—will be set for other nutrient groups, including antioxidants, macronutrients, trace minerals, and fiber.

For a comprehensive listing of the content of vitamins, minerals, phytonutrients, macronutrients (protein, fat, carbohydrates), fiber, and calories in various food sources (fruits, vegetables, grains, high-protein foods, dairy foods, sweeteners, beverages, fats, and oils) for all age groups refer to the USDA's nutrient Data Laboratory home page, www.nal.usda.gov/fnic/foodcomp.

As nutritional research becomes more influential in mainstream medicine, it's becoming routine for M.D.s to prescribe high doses of vitamins and minerals to address specific conditions or diseases. For example, high doses of calcium are often prescribed for women to prevent osteoporosis, high doses of folic acid are often prescribed for women as part of good pre- and postnatal care, and people who suffer from anemia are usually given iron supplements.

The Total Health Approach to Vitamins and Minerals

1. **Eat a protein-rich, favorable-carbohydrate diet.** The best way to make sure your body is supplied with a continuing source of essential micronutrients is to eat a wide variety of foods. It bears repeating that no vitamin or mineral supplement can compensate for the lack of eating a properly balanced, protein-rich, favorable-carbohydrate diet. That's why they're called vitamin and mineral *supplements*—not replacements.

2. **Do no harm!** Do not take megadoses of vitamins or minerals unless they are prescribed by your doctor to treat a specific deficiency. Some vitamin advocates go so far as to recommend massive doses of certain vitamins to ward off ailments ranging from cancer to impotence. The FDA and mainstream medicine regard these vitamin fads as quackery—and often dangerous. For example, large amounts of vitamin A can contribute to liver damage. Excess doses of vitamin D can contribute to kidney damage. Iron, zinc, chromium, and selenium can be toxic at just five times the RDA. The most common cause of poisoning deaths among children is adult-strength iron supplements.

3. **Use vitamin and mineral supplements as nutritional insurance.** The Total Health program provides your body with the essential micronutrients it needs from two sources: the food you eat and a high-quality vitamin and mineral supplement.

Choosing the Right Vitamin and Mineral Supplements

It's important to consider the following ingredients when choosing high-quality vitamin and mineral supplements. If you're confused about what kind of supplement to purchase, refer to Appendix B, "Recommended Products," in the back of the book for my top recommendations of quality vitamin and mineral supplements.

Antioxidants

Antioxidants protect your body from exposure to everyday environmental factors such as cigarette smoke, air pollution, and sunlight, which stimulate free radical production. Free radicals—natural by-products of cell metabolism, the process by which cells use oxygen to create energy—are chemically reactive oxygen molecules that are missing an electron. Because electrons prefer to travel in pairs, free radicals aggressively steal electrons from healthy molecules. The electron-stealing chain reaction that results produces compounds that cause cellular damage.

Scientists estimate that each cell in the body may be pounded with as many as 10,000 free radical hits a day! Your body does its best to counter free radicals naturally, but over time free radical buildup takes its toll. It's no wonder that many scientists link damage by free radicals to cancer, heart disease, cataracts, and premature aging.

Antioxidants counter free radical damage by supplying extra electrons that bind with and stabilize free radical molecules. Antioxidant-rich foods and supplements provide the body with the ammunition it needs to fend off the nonstop free radical bombardment. Some of the most commonly known antioxidant nutrients are vitamins A, C, and E.

Phytonutrients

Phytonutrients, or phytochemicals, are nutrients from plants that promote a variety of beneficial functions. Many exhibit powerful antioxidant properties. Scientists are working feverishly to mine the largely unexplored potential that phytonutrients hold for medicine. Some of the research has revealed amazing possibilities.

One class of phytonutrients found in grape seeds, for example, exhibits antioxidant properties in the body for up to three days. More important, it is able to cross the blood-brain barrier. Brain tissue is particularly susceptible to free radical–induced oxidation. This phytonutrient also inhibits enzymes that break down vitamins C and E into less useful nutrients.

Some of the best phytonutrients are proanthocyanidins (found in grape seed extract), sulforaphane (found in broccoli extract), and lycopene (found in tomato extract).

Chelated Minerals and Trace Elements

Dietary minerals and trace elements support biochemical processes that help your body burn fat, build muscle, strengthen bones, promote healing, and deliver oxygen to your cells. Proper absorption, or bioavailability, is essential to effective mineral and trace element supplementation. Minerals and trace elements are more rapidly absorbed by the intestinal tract when they are chelated—or wrapped—in an amino acid coating. Chelated calcium, for example, is absorbed sixty times as effectively as the calcium in milk.

Enzymes

All biochemical reactions are started or accelerated by a special class of protein molecules called enzymes. One of the best-known enzyme supplements is lactase, which helps people who are lactose intolerant or unable to digest dairy products properly.

Even though lactase is a helpful enzyme, as a supplement it's normally used before the consumption of dairy products only by those who lack the natural enzyme lactase.

Bromelain is another enzyme that is getting a lot of attention for its digestive benefits. It's found in particularly high concentrations in pineapple. Bromelain is also being studied for its therapeutic value in treating severe bruises, inflammation, and soft tissue injuries.

Pancreatic enzymes, such as amylase, protease, and lipase, are used to treat malabsorption syndromes, when the body's ability to digest a variety of nutrients is greatly impaired. They're also essential in breaking down proteins, fats, and carbohydrates for proper digestion.

Herbs

In general, the side effects of herbal products are minimal. Many consumers are entranced by the designation "all natural" and thus tend to believe that all herbal products are safe. They don't think of herbs as drugs.

Consumers should be advised by providers of medicinal herbs to observe the proper dosage recommendations and stop taking an herbal product if any adverse reactions occur. There isn't much information on herb–drug interactions, so people who are also taking prescription medications should be cautious. The *Botanical Safety Handbook,* published by the American Herbal Products Association, contains labeling recommendations for 700 herbs commonly used in the United States.

Herbal products have become more popular as consumers seek relief from common symptoms from sources other than their physicians. Therefore, the majority of the responsibility for patients' safety will fall on doctors and the pharmaceutical industry.

Medical doctors are now recognizing the widespread use of herbal products among their patients, and more clinical studies are under way. Physicians, as a rule, aren't very familiar with the herbal agents but will benefit their patients by being able to discuss these products with them.

TOTAL HEALTH SUCCESS STORY

Feeling Great in a Size 8

JUDY A.
Account executive

AGE: 63
HEIGHT: 5 FEET, 4 INCHES
TOTAL HEALTH START DATE: NOVEMBER 1999
START WEIGHT: 149 POUNDS
AFTER WEIGHT: 125 POUNDS
TOTAL WEIGHT LOSS: 24 POUNDS
START BODY FAT PERCENTAGE: 38%
AFTER BODY FAT PERCENTAGE: 28.6%
START FAT POUNDS: 56
AFTER FAT POUNDS: 35
TOTAL POUNDS OF FAT LOSS: 21
START DRESS OR PANTS SIZE: 16
AFTER DRESS OR PANTS SIZE: 8

Judy A. before

Judy A. after

The future belongs to those who prepare for it!

In 1999, I decided I didn't want to be 60, size 16, and unhealthy. The day before Thanksgiving I went on Dr. Markham's Total Health plan, and by Christmas was a perfect size 10. By my sixtieth birthday, in September 2000, I was a size 8.

I believe it was Madeline, a coworker, who first introduced me to the Total Health plan. There were about thirty of us following the Total Health program at the time. I especially remember my coworker Jackie—she looked as if she'd lost half of her body. You couldn't even recognize her.

I was really impressed with my coworkers who were losing weight, looking healthy, and smiling all the time. My middle-age spread was getting the best of me, and looking at pictures of myself was very depressing. What did I have to lose other than a few dress sizes?

Feeling good and healthy was also a priority. My doctor was impressed with my yearly physical stats when I went in for my checkup, and she asked me what I had been doing. She thought it was wonderful. All of my numbers were perfect.

The Total Health plan maintenance is a way of life. I am not a slave to my diet because I simply put what I have learned about what I eat to work. The Golden Rule: Never eat a carb without a protein.

Still feeling great in a size 8.

It is the pharmaceutical (drug) companies' responsibility to educate the physicians about what popular herbs may cause adverse reactions when taken with certain medications. Physicians will also have to have better screening forms and processes to determine what kind of herbs their patients may be taking before prescribing certain medications.

GOT WATER?

Why You Need to Drink More

Are you drinking enough water? If you're like most of my patients, the answer is: not as much as you know you should.

Water helps your body digest food, absorb nutrients, and transport those nutrients throughout your body. It's also a vital part of your body's waste removal system. Without adequate amounts of water, your body becomes dehydrated and cannot function properly.

More acute cases of dehydration can cause fatigue, nausea, and dementia. Severe cases often lead to heat exhaustion, heatstroke, and even death.

You don't have to run for hours in the summer sun to become dehydrated. In fact, most of us live in a chronic state of mild dehydration. Sure, we drink water every day, but not enough. Or we think that drinking water-based fluids, such as coffee, tea, or soda, is the same as drinking water. It's not. Coffee, tea, and many sodas contain caffeine, a diuretic that dehydrates your body.

Make no mistake: dehydration, however mild, can lead to serious health problems. If you aren't drinking enough water, over time your kidneys will pay the price. Your kidneys are an integral part of your body's purification system. Their main job is to clean your blood of toxins and metabolic wastes. And to function properly, they rely on a steady and sufficient flow of water.

The less water you drink, the more stress your kidneys suffer and the less efficient they become. Over time, this chronic abuse can contribute to health problems, ranging from increased likeliness of illness to painful kidney stones to kidney failure.

The bottom line: Take care of your kidneys by drinking plenty of water.

Flush Away Excess Body Fat

Drinking lots of water doesn't wash away body fat, but it does help your kidneys flush out the metabolic waste that is generated by burning excess body fat. Some of this waste is partially burned fat, which passes from your body in stool or urine. So the more water you drink, the more urine you generate and the more fat your body gets rid of.

How Much Water Do You Need?

The general medical consensus is about two quarts, or six to eight glasses a day. You need more if you exercise regularly or live in a hot climate.

The Best Way to Monitor Your Water Intake

Don't watch the amount of liquid going into your body, watch the liquid that's going out. Take note of the frequency and color of your urine. As a general rule, you're drinking enough if you urinate regularly and the color is clear or pale yellow. If you urinate infrequently or the color is bright or dark yellow, your body needs more water.

Water and Total Health Tips

Here's another reason to drink enough water: Along with storing fat, high insulin levels also promote water retention. As your Total Health program stabilizes your insulin levels, you'll start to shed this excess water. To stay hydrated, you need to replenish your body's water supply. Drinking the right amount of water every day may take some practice. Here are some tips to get you into the hydration habit:

• **Start your day with an eight-ounce glass of water.** Your body is always dehydrated after six to eight hours without water. The sooner you hydrate, the better and more alert you'll feel—even before that first cup of coffee!

• **Drink an eight-ounce glass of water before breakfast, lunch, and dinner.** Drinking water before meals tends to take the edge off hunger.

• **Reduce your consumption of coffee and other caffeinated beverages to one or two cups a day.** Aside from its diuretic quality, coffee can stimulate excess insulin production. Replace those extra cups of coffee with hot water. Add lemon for flavor, if you like. Herbal teas are also okay. Many people have discovered that sipping hot water or herbal tea is a remarkably effective way to wean themselves off caffeine. Reduce your caffeine consumption gradually to minimize the headaches and mood swings that often accompany caffeine withdrawal.

• **Ask yourself if you're thirsty.** Chances are you're much thirstier than you realize. Asking the question forces you to become aware of your thirst. But you can't do anything about it unless you have water on hand. When water is out of sight, it's out of mind. That's why you should . . .

• **Take water with you.** Next time you're in the grocery store, buy a flat of 16-ounce disposable water bottles. Take one with you wherever you go—in the car, to work, on errands, when you go for a walk. When the bottle is empty, refill it. One way to keep track of your water intake is to place four rubber bands around the bottle. Each time you finish 16 ounces, take off a rubber band.

• **Get bubbly.** These days, supermarkets have entire aisles dedicated to bottled water products. For variety, put some plain or flavored carbonated water in your cart. Look for orange-, lemon-, or lime-flavored sparkling water. Stay away from carbonated water flavored with juice. You want the bubbles, not the extra sugar.

• **Monitor your water output.** The best indication that you're drinking more water is that you urinate more frequently. Don't think of this as an inconvenience. Think of it as a sign that you're helping your body's natural purification system keep you healthy.

FIBER FACTS

Let's do a little word association. If I say "fiber," what's the first thought that pops into your head? If you said "constipation," you're being honest. Most of us think of fiber as the stuff that keeps our bowels "regular"—what Mom and Dad used to refer to less delicately as roughage.

What Is Fiber?

Fiber is the part of plant food that your body can't digest. Actually, there are five different kinds of fiber. Nutritionists divide them into two main categories: soluble and insoluble.

- **The soluble fibers are pectin and gum.** They're found in foods such as beans, oats, and citrus fruits. Soluble fibers dissolve and thicken in water.
- **The insoluble fibers are cellulose, hemicellulose, and lignin.** They are found in foods such as wheat bran, nuts, seeds, and fruits. Insoluble fibers include the outer coating of grains and the skins of fruits and vegetables. Insoluble fibers don't dissolve in water.

Why Fiber Is Good for You

Thanks to increasing scientific study, fiber is getting a lot more respect than its well-deserved reputation as a natural remedy for constipation. The medical community now recognizes fiber as an essential dietary component with long-term health benefits. This is because:

- **Fiber helps prevent hemorrhoids.** Hemorrhoids are the painful swelling of veins near the anus, most often caused by strained bowel movements. Fiber softens and adds bulk to the stool, making it easier to pass.
- **Fiber reduces the risk of heart disease by lowering cholesterol levels.** Fiber binds to cholesterol and evacuates it in the stool before its absorption into the bloodstream.
- **Fiber helps regulate insulin levels.** Fiber diminishes the body's insulin response by inhibiting the absorption of glucose into the bloodstream.
- **Fiber may reduce the risk of certain cancers.** For years, researchers have said that a high-fiber diet may reduce the risk of colon, rectal, and breast cancer. A number of explanations have been offered. One popular theory holds that fiber speeds up the passage of harmful waste through the intestines, minimizing its absorption and contact with intestinal cells.

How Much Fiber Do You Need?

The general medical consensus is between 25 and 40 grams daily. Most Americans get less than half that amount. That's why your Total Health program makes it easy to get all the fiber you need. You just don't get it from carbohydrate-loaded food choices that stimulate excess insulin production and fat storage.

On the Total Health program you can get your fiber in several ways:

• **Choose carbohydrates in the form of fiber-rich fruits and vegetables.** For a list of fruits and vegetables that qualify as fiber-rich carbohydrates, see the "Macronutrient Units list on page 84.

• **If you must eat bread or pasta, limit the amount and choose whole grains.**

• **Take your nutritional supplements.** They complement your protein-rich, favorable-carbohydrate eating program.

• **Take a fiber supplement,** such as Metamucil or other over-the-counter fiber supplements. Refer to Appendix B, "Recommended Products," for my top recommendations.

• **A final tip: Increase your fiber intake gradually!** Too much fiber can cause gas or diarrhea. To avoid these natural side effects, drink plenty of water.

Digestive Disorders: The "Silo Syndrome"

Growing up in the farm country of Wisconsin has once again come in handy! It's given us the term "silo syndrome."

One of the first things I advise patients to eliminate during the beginning stages of the Total Health weight loss program is high-glycemic carbohydrates, such as pasta (made with flour and water), starchy white rice and potatoes, and excessive amounts of grains—all the types of carbohydrates that convert into sugar very rapidly.

Many of my patients who suffered from indigestion and other more serious digestive disorders also ate excessive amounts of these types of carbohydrates. Many of these same patients were also taking prescription medications prescribed by their gastroenterologists to help alleviate the symptoms of indigestion.

Within weeks of eliminating the flour and grains, their symptoms of indigestion started to fade—so much that many of the patients were able to reduce and even eliminate their medications for digestive disorders.

Upon further clinical evaluation and exploration of my Wisconsin roots, the answer was clear! The same process that takes place inside the tall cylinders (silos) standing next to the barns on the farms of Wisconsin was also taking place in the stomachs of my patients—a process called *fermentation*.

When farmers fill the silos with feed corn to feed their livestock over the winter, it starts to ferment. This fermentation process gives off powerful nitrogenous gases. These nitrogenous gases are so strong that farmers will sometimes be overcome by the gases, pass out, and even die. This happens when the unsuspecting farmer gets inside the silo to dislodge feed corn that has become stuck in the grain chute.

These same powerful nitrogenous gases build up in our stomachs and digestive tracts as a result of the fermentation of flour, starches, and other grains during the normal digestive process. It's these same gases that eventually irritate the lining of our stomachs and digestive tracts, causing indigestion and more serious digestive disorders.

Hence, the term "silo syndrome" was born!

SWEETENERS

Artificial sweeteners, or sugar substitutes, have been on the market for years as tabletop sweeteners and used by the food industry to sweeten foods and beverages. They've opened a whole new world for people from low-carb followers to diabetics who want to enjoy sweets without adversely affecting their weight and blood sugar level.

The use of various nutritive (caloric) and nonnutritive (noncaloric) sweeteners is acceptable in the management of diabetes and weight management by most health professionals. Regardless of their popularity and availability, health professionals agree that these products can be a part of a healthy diet, but that doesn't mean you can freely consume desserts, candies, and beverages containing them.

One of the first questions most people ask is "Are these sweeteners safe to consume?" In order for sweeteners to be offered on supermarket shelves, they have to be approved by the FDA. This means they've been proven safe for human consumption. Women who are pregnant or breast-feeding should talk to their physician about the use of artificial sweeteners. However, some people are still not comfortable using artificial sweeteners and prefer to use "real sugar" in their diets, even though this will inhibit their weight loss due to its high carbohydrate content.

Sweeteners are separated into two categories: *nutritive* (containing calories) and *nonnutritive* (containing no calories).

- *Nutritive sweeteners* are broken down by the body and therefore provide energy, but they do not contribute any other essential nutrients.
- *Nonnutritive sweeteners* do not provide any energy to the diet.

Nutritive (Caloric) Sweeteners

The nutritive sweeteners can be broken down into two subgroups: sugar and sugar alcohols.

Sugar

The term "sugar" is used to refer to a class of nutritive sweeteners or high-glycemic carbohydrates with a sweet taste. These include sucrose, fructose, lactose, and glucose. Although there is a wide variety of sugars in the form of sucrose (common table sugar), raw sugar, turbinado sugar, brown sugar, honey, and corn syrup, there is no significant difference in their nutritional content or the calories each provides.

Therefore, other than choosing natural, unprocessed forms of raw sugar over processed white sugar, one has no advantage over another.

SUCROSE

Sucrose or table sugar is a carbohydrate derived from sugarcane or sugar beets. It's the most commonly used sugar. Although many of us have a desire for sweetness due to our brain's need for glucose, as previously discussed, sugar is not essential to health.

FRUCTOSE

Fructose is a naturally occurring sugar found in fruits and vegetables. It contains up to 40 percent fewer calories than table sugar and is up to 40 percent sweeter. Fructose is most effective as a sweetening agent in high-acid and cold foods, such as citrus drinks.

Fructose travels mainly to the liver and can be used there without the need for insulin. In the absence of insulin, fructose can be converted to glucose in the liver and therefore can contribute to an increase in blood glucose rather than being stored as glycogen. Unlike sucrose and glucose, which cause rapid changes in the blood glucose level, fructose is absorbed more slowly and causes fewer changes in the blood sugar level due to being metabolized in the liver.

Fructose-sweetened products can still make a significant contribution to caloric intake, and therefore fructose can't be considered a sweetener to be used freely.

Sugar Alcohols

The term "sugar alcohols" is used to refer to a class of nutritive sweeteners also called polyols, which are neither sugars nor alcohol. These include sorbitol, mannitol, xylitol, lactitol, HSH (hydrogenated starch hydrolysate), maltitol, isomalt, and erythritol.

Sugar alcohols have little effect on the blood sugar level because they're digested and absorbed much more slowly. Although they contain "zero net carbs," meaning they don't have to be counted as carbohydrates, they still contain some calories.

Excessive consumption of low-carb products containing some types of sugar alcohols may lead to abdominal cramping, gas, and laxative effects. Therefore, excessive consumption of low-carb products sweetened with sugar alcohols is not recommended. Moderation is certainly the key to the consumption of any kind of processed snack, food, or beverage.

SORBITOL, MANNITOL, AND XYLITOL
Sorbitol and mannitol are naturally found in small amounts in some fruits and vegetables and are used as sweeteners in many products. Sorbitol is approximately 60 percent as sweet as sucrose, and mannitol is 70 percent as sweet; therefore more of each must be used to reach the same level of sweetness. Depending upon the gastrointestinal sensitivity of the individual, mannitol can cause diarrhea and abdominal complaints if more than 20 grams are consumed daily; for sorbitol the amount is about 50 grams per day.

Xylitol, also derived from fruits and vegetables, can be found in carrots, lettuce, and strawberries.

LACTITOL
Lactitol is currently used as a bulk sweetener. It was first used as a sweetener in the 1980s and is only about 40 percent as sweet as sucrose. It has half the calories as sucrose, with about 2 calories per gram.

HSH (HYDROGENATED STARCH HYDROLYSATE)
Hydrogenated starch hydrolysate, which also goes by the trade name Lycasin, is derived from corn, wheat, and potato starch. Further processing

yields a combination product of sorbitol, maltitol, and hydrogenated saccharides.

Maltitol

Maltitol is made from the hydrogenation of maltose, which is derived from starch. It's 90 percent as sweet as sucrose and low in calories. Abdominal cramping, gas, and laxative effects are often experienced when maltitol is consumed in excess of 15 grams per day.

Isomalt

Isomalt is a great-tasting sweetener with the same sweetness as sugar. It was discovered in the 1960s and is created by mixing mannitol and sorbitol. It's used in a wide variety of products from hard candies to cough drops.

Erythritol

Erythritol is low in calories, 70 percent as sweet as sucrose, and doesn't have the unpleasant laxative side effects of other sugar alcohols due to its rapid absorption. It's naturally present in fruits such as pears, melons, and grapes, along with mushrooms and fermented foods such as wine, soy sauce, and cheese. Due to its limited side effects and only 0.2 calories per gram, erythritol is the "shining star" of sugar alcohols.

Nonnutritive (Noncaloric) Sweeteners

Sucralose (Splenda®)

Sucralose is the common name for the only calorie-free sweetener made from sugar. It's created through a patented process that alters the sugar molecule. It has no aftertaste and looks and tastes like sugar. It isn't broken down in the body and therefore provides no calories. Sucralose is about 600 times as sweet as sugar.

Due to its stability and pleasant taste, it can be used by consumers and manufacturers in a wide variety of foods and beverages. These include baked goods, drinks, frozen desserts, chewing gum, milk products, salad dressings, tabletop sweeteners, and alcoholic beverages.

Splenda is available in two tabletop forms: granular and packet. The granular form measures, pours, and can be used like real sugar, even in cooking and baking. Each packet contains the equivalent of 2 teaspoons of sugar.

Acesulfame K (Ace-K)

Acesulfame K (Ace-K) is a calorie-free sweetener discovered in 1965. It's almost 200 times as sweet as sucrose and is sold under the brand name Sunett. It's used in thousands of products, offering low-calorie, low-sugar foods to incorporate into a healthy diet. It gives a sweet taste with no lingering aftertaste. Ace-K is also sodium-free and does not promote tooth decay.

Ace-K can be blended with nutritive sweeteners. The blending of nutritive and nonnutritive sweeteners produces the desired level of sweetness in the product while using substantially less of the individual sweeteners.

More and more food companies are using sweetener combinations because blending provides advantages for both the food manufacturer and the consumer. The food company is able to use less total sweetener while providing the consumer with an improved taste in the end product.

Ace-K contains the sulfur atom, but there is no danger that people who are allergic to sulfa drugs or products containing sulfites will have a reaction because its properties are different from products containing sulfites and from sulfa drugs.

Ace-K isn't metabolized by the body and therefore has no caloric value. It's rapidly absorbed after ingestion and is excreted unchanged in the urine.

Stevia (STEE-vee-uh)

Stevia is a type of South American shrub, and *Stevia rebaudiana* leaves have been used for centuries by native peoples in Paraguay and Brazil to sweeten their beverages. Stevioside, the main ingredient in stevia, is virtually calorie-free and 300 times sweeter than table sugar. However, the scientific panel that reviews the safety of food ingredients for the European Union concluded that stevioside isn't acceptable as a sweetener because of unresolved concerns about its toxicity. Therefore, the herb has not been approved as an additive for sweetening foods in the United States and is currently sold as a dietary supplement only.

Other studies have shown stevia to be safe for human consumption, and it's currently being used in other parts of the world as a sweetener for pickles, dried foods, soy sauce, fruit juices, soft drinks, and gum.

Saccharin (Hermesetas, Sweet'N Low)

Saccharin was the first man-made calorie-free sugar substitute. Saccharin is 300 to 400 times as sweet as sucrose and is found in many foods and beverages. Scientific studies have found no conclusive link between saccharin and bladder cancer, although there is a need for more research.

ASPARTAME (EQUAL, NUTRASWEET)

Aspartame is 180 times as sweet as sugar and is used as a sweetener in a variety of foods and beverages. It goes by the trade names Equal and Nutra-Sweet, which are available in packets as low-calorie tabletop sweeteners.

Aspartame is derived from two naturally occurring amino acids, aspartic acid and phenylalanine. However, because of the minimal number of calories provided by aspartame, it's grouped with the nonnutritive sweeteners.

Unlike sucrose, aspartame's commercial use is limited as it does break down and lose its sweetness when used in baking at high temperatures or when combined with acidic foods. Therefore, aspartame is used as a sweetener and flavor enhanced only in certain foods.

The question of the stability of aspartame in liquid during long-term storage has also been raised. The FDA has determined that although long-term storage may result in a marginally acceptable product from a taste standpoint, it would not lead to an unsafe product.

Aspartame is not known to have harmful effects for most people. However, some individuals who suffer from a hereditary disease known as phenylketonuria must control their intake of phenylalanine, one of the amino acids in aspartame.

There have been many public safety concerns about aspartame, as well as some reported reactions to the product. Confirmation of reactions to food ingredients and food additives is always difficult, especially when not diagnosed by a physician specializing in food allergies. The FDA is closely monitoring such complaints. The labeling requirements for food additives are being improved to enable those who wish to avoid specific substances to do so. Some people claim to be particularly sensitive to the ingestion of aspartame and experience a wide variety of mild nonspecific symptoms. Headaches, irritability, and failure to lose weight or to control the blood sugar level have all been reported.

Summary

The benefits of the use of artificial sweeteners have been proven by the variety of foods available, particularly for people with diabetes and followers

TOTAL HEALTH SUCCESS STORY

A British World War II Veteran and Still
Going Strong

JOE L.
Retired engineer

AGE: 80
HEIGHT: 5 FEET, 6 INCHES
TOTAL HEALTH START DATE: MARCH 2002
START WEIGHT: 202 POUNDS
AFTER WEIGHT: 162 POUNDS
TOTAL WEIGHT LOSS: 40 POUNDS
START BODY FAT PERCENTAGE: 39.2%
AFTER BODY FAT PERCENTAGE: 33.3%
START FAT POUNDS: 79.5
AFTER FAT POUNDS: 52
TOTAL POUNDS OF FAT LOSS: 27.5

Joe L. before

Joe L. after

After twenty-five years of marriage, my daughter and son-in-law were both overweight and decided to follow the principles of Dr. Markham's Total Health protein-rich, favorable-carbohydrate way of eating. Using the daily food menus as outlined in his book, they both started to lose weight and feel better. I watched my daughter go on to lose 56 pounds and my son-in-law 90 pounds.

They were so successful that my daughter encouraged me to consider making the same changes in my eating habits. I was 78 years old at the time and had to walk with the aid of a walker due to back strain and weak legs. My wife had passed on several years before, and I had sort of given up on being concerned about my health.

I served my native country of England in World War II as a pilot. My wife, who served in the Royal Navy as a secretary for Winston Churchill, and I were married for more than fifty years before her passing. We also raised four wonderful children together. And despite enjoying my grandchildren, I felt I had pretty much lived a full and complete life. Fortunately, my daughter had other ideas in mind and introduced me to Dr. Doug's Total Health plan.

When I first came to see Dr. Markham, I weighed more than 200 pounds and came through his office door using a walker. The combination of eating English Yorkshire tea cakes every morning for breakfast and lack of physical activity had definitely contributed to my excessive weight gain.

I started adopting Dr. Doug's eating recommendations of cottage cheese with fruit for breakfast; 4 ounces of chicken, fish, or lean beef with vegetables for lunch and dinner; and my favorite snack of Dannon Light Yogurt at my scheduled snack time. The pounds soon started to disappear.

After 20 pounds of weight loss, I was able to walk without the use of my walker, and I even started Dr. Markham's 30-minute circuit training workout. When my son called from Canada to see how I was doing, he was shocked when I told him I was exercising. He's always been an exercise enthusiast and was overjoyed by my newfound health success!

Probably the most exciting thing about my increased strength, endurance, and energy level is that I was able to take my daughter Josephine to England for her very first time to attend my sister's fiftieth wedding anniversary. I'd thought I would never have the opportunity to take her to England because I was too old and my health was failing. Tears came to both of our eyes when I was able to show her the house where she was born in Watford, England.

Now, at 80 years old, I continue to eat right, exercise, and enjoy my family and the companionship of my loyal dog, Kuno.

---

of a low-carb lifestyle. The possible risk presented by an individual sweetener can be minimized by using it in moderation.

Current evidence indicates that the use of sweeteners available to consumers in moderation is safe and not associated with any serious risks. It's important that the public have a choice of various nutritive and nonnutritive sweeteners, with safe and reasonable guidelines on how to use each type.

As new sweeteners become available, they must undergo the same rigorous testing as previously approved sweeteners, and research into the possible risks of long-term uses of nutritive and nonnutritive sweeteners should be continued.

FOOD PREPARATION TIPS

Hot or iced caffelatte: Keep your drink sugar-free. If available, you may sweeten your latte with a shot of sugar-free syrup.

Meat, poultry, and fish: Cook meat by grilling, broiling, baking, or stir-frying.

Salad dressing: Use olive oil and vinegar. Olive oil is an excellent source of linoleic acid, an essential fatty acid. You may also use regular dressings such as ranch dressing, but check the carbohydrate content on the label. Stay away from low-fat and no-fat dressings; they're loaded with sugar.

Vegetables: You may melt a pat of real butter over your veggies. Do not use margarine because margarine contains partially hydrogenated vegetable oil, a source of unfavorable trans-fatty acids.

Yogurt: Use yogurt sweetened with a sugar substitute. If you don't like artificial sweeteners, flavor half a cup of plain yogurt with vanilla extract and natural sweetener stevia or Splenda or your favorite sugar-free syrup flavor to taste.

Part III

Eating Your Way to
Total Health

PULLING IT ALL TOGETHER

We've talked about the connection between the food you eat, your blood sugar levels, and the hormonal response to burn or store body fat. How does this work in the real world?

Whether your goal is to reduce body fat, increase your mental and physical productivity, or reduce your chances of illness, the Total Health protein-rich, favorable-carbohydrate way of eating is for you. To get started on a protein-rich, favorable-carbohydrate way of eating, the first thing you have to do is figure out your *daily protein requirement*—in other words, how much protein your body needs on a daily basis. Remember, the Total Health plan is not a "high-protein" diet; it's a healthy way of eating based on your body's daily protein needs.

Your daily protein requirement is determined by your percentage of lean body mass multiplied by your ideal percentage body fat. "Lean body mass" refers to the percentage of your body that isn't fat. This is basically your bone and muscle weight. The fastest and most accurate way to determine your lean body mass is to use an electrical impedance body fat analyzer.

There are many different types of battery-operated handheld and scale types of body fat analyzers on the market today. They can be found in the bath departments of department stores, fitness stores, etc. Refer to Appendix C, "Exercise Resources" for my top recommendations for body fat analyzers.

I'm in favor of determining people's ideal and healthy weight based on their ideal percentage body fat. I personally don't feel that the body mass index (BMI) is the most accurate way to properly determine someone's health risk. This is due to the BMI's inability to take into account an individual's natural amount of muscle mass. This holds true especially when evaluating the health risks of body builders and athletes.

A BMI of 19 to 24.9 is considered a minimal to low health risk, 25 to 29.9 is considered overweight, with a moderate health risk, and 30 or higher is considered obese with higher health risks associated with heart disease, stroke, and adult-onset diabetes. Extreme obesity is above 40.

The following chart reflects your *ideal body fat percentage* based on your age and gender:

IDEAL BODY FAT		
Age (Years)	Males	Females
10–30	12–18%	20–26%
31–40	13–19%	21–27%
41–50	14–20%	22–28%
51–60	16–20%	22–30%
61 and above	17–21%	22–31%

The way your lean body mass is determined is to subtract your *fat pounds* (calculated on the body fat analyzer) from your total weight. So if you weighed 150 pounds and you had 50 pounds of fat, your lean body mass (fat-free body weight) would be 100 pounds.

How to Determine Your Ideal Weight

To calculate your *ideal weight,* simply multiply your lean body mass by your ideal body fat percentage and add the total to your lean body mass. Thus, if you are a 25-year-old female with 100 pounds of lean body mass and want to reach the high end of your ideal percentage body fat of 26 percent, your ideal weight would be 126 pounds.

How to Calculate Your Daily Protein Requirement

Once we've determined your lean body mass, we multiply your lean body mass by your daily activity index. This means how active you are, which is anything from 0.5, or "couch potato" material, to 0.9, which indicates someone who exercises daily.

Activity Levels

1. **Sedentary:** No physical activity; protein need is *0.5 gram* per pound of lean body mass.
2. **Moderately active:** 20–30 minutes of exercise, two to three times per week; protein need is *0.6 gram* per pound of lean body mass.
3. **Active:** 30 minutes of exercise, three to five times per week; protein need is *0.7 gram* per pound of lean body mass.
4. **Very Active:** Vigorous exercise for an hour or more five or more times per week; protein need is *0.8 gram* per pound of lean body mass.
5. **Athlete:** Athlete in training, twice-daily heavy workouts for an hour or more; protein need is *0.9 grams* per pound of lean body mass.

So, if your lean body mass is 100 pounds and you are in the "active" activity level category, you would multiply 0.7 by 100 for a daily protein requirement of 70 grams of protein per day.

A Simple Alternative to Calculating Your Daily Protein Requirement

If you're confused about the previous information and don't have access to a body fat analyzer, we have provided the following choices for your approximate daily protein requirement according to your body frame size.

To determine your body frame size, place yourself into the following body frame category according to your height:

TYPE OF BODY FRAME

Petite: 5 feet, 1 inch and below
Small: 5 feet, 2 inches to 5 feet, 5 inches

Medium: 5 feet, 6 inches to 5 feet, 9 inches
Large: 5 feet, 10 inches and above

PROTEIN REQUIREMENT PER DAY*

Petite: 60–70 grams
Small: 70–80 grams
Medium: 80–90 grams
Large: 90–100 grams

Simply match your body frame size with the appropriate Total Health Protein-Rich, Favorable-Carbohydrate Menu Options beginning on page 86.

HOW TO USE YOUR TOTAL HEALTH MENU OPTIONS

Timing Is Everything

Remember the idea that food is a drug? One key to using drugs effectively is to make sure you take your medicine at regular intervals to maintain an even dosage level. The same principle applies to the Total Health eating program.

The key to regulating your blood sugars and burning body fat consistently is to eat every 3½ to 4 hours. This interval promotes optimal metabolism and blood sugar regulation. So I put my patients on a schedule of breakfast at 8 A.M., lunch around noon, a snack around 3:30 P.M., dinner around 7 P.M., and an optional bedtime snack around 11 P.M.

Here's how your daily protein and carbohydrate requirements should be portioned out over the course of a day:

• If you're at your ideal body fat and weight, you can eat a one-to-one ratio of protein to carbohydrates to maintain your weight. For example, if you are in the large body frame category, your daily protein requirement would be approximately 100 grams of protein to 100 grams of carbohydrate per day.

• If you want to put your body into a fat-burning mode of a moderate

* If you exercise three times per week or more, add 10 grams of protein per day.

amount of weight loss of about 2 to 3 pounds a week or about 10 pounds per month, you would limit yourself to 40 grams of carbohydrate per day, although you would still eat 100 grams of protein per day.

So for a fat-burning or weight loss mode you would consume the 100 grams of protein over the course of the day at the suggested mealtimes of every 3½ to 4 hours. Therefore, you would have approximately 28 grams of protein each at breakfast, lunch, and dinner, with about 7 to 10 grams at your two snack times. You would also break down the 40 grams of carbohydrates over the course of the day by eating 10 grams of carbohydrates at breakfast, lunch, and dinner, with 5 grams at your two snack times.

To avoid losing weight too fast and to reduce potential uncomfortable side effects and maintaining a healthy rate of weight loss, I start all my patients at 40 grams of carbohydrates per day.

If you follow your customized Total Health Protein-Rich, Favorable-Carbohydrate Menu Options and have a large body frame, you can expect to lose 2 to 4 pounds of excess weight the first week or 8 to 10 pounds per month. If you have less weight to lose or a small or petite body frame, you can expect to lose 1 to 2 pounds of excess weight a week or 6 to 8 pounds per month.

If you experience a prolonged period of little or no weight loss, your customized menu should be adjusted to "jump-start" renewed weight loss. If you experience such a plateau, simply cut your carbohydrate consumption at each meal in half. If this doesn't work, you may want to consider the following "12 Tips for Breaking a Weight Loss Plateau."

---

12 TIPS FOR BREAKING A WEIGHT LOSS PLATEAU

1. Watch out for unsuspected carbohydrate sources. Don't forget about chewing gum, cough drops, and breath mints. Many times we forget that 1–2 grams of carbohydrates per stick of gum, breath mint, etc., can add up by the end of the day.

2. Make sure you're eating enough protein at each meal. You may not be eating enough protein at each meal. Remember to adhere to your daily protein requirement based on your body frame size as outlined in the Total Health plan.

3. Be sure to eat at your scheduled times. A frequent eating schedule will provide a constant source of energy without the insulin rebound. Remember to eat every 3½ to 4 hours, and don't skip meals or snacks! When you don't eat, your body will go into a conservation mode, and you will quit losing weight.

4. Reduce your carbohydrate intake. You may need to reduce your carbohydrate intake even further in the beginning if your body is resistant to weight loss.

5. Increase your exercise. Following the exercise recommendations in **Part IV, "Exercise: How to Get Started and Why"** (page 113) will help to increase weight loss.

6. Check the label on your vitamins. Certain vitamin mixtures may contain carbohydrates. Colloidal or liquid mineral mixtures often include a juice formula containing sugars. Be sure to check the carbohydrate amounts on the label.

7. Avoid excessive use of alcohol. Even though I recommend distilled spirits or hard alcohol over beer and wine because of their zero carbohydrate content, it still contains calories. Excessive alcohol consumption can stimulate an insulin response, slowing your weight loss efforts. Remember to drink alcohol in moderation.

8. Be aware of medications. Several different types of medications, from HRT (hormone replacement therapy) to serotonin-producing antidepressants such as Prozac and others, may lead to weight gain. Here are a few medications also on the weight gain list: birth control pills, diuretics, antihistamines, anti-inflammatory drugs, blood sugar–lowering medications, and antibiotics.

9. Avoid excessive sodium intake. Check the labels of foods for sodium content and refrain from excessive use of salt, which may cause fluid retention.

10. Exercise portion control. You may be eating too much protein at each meal, or the fat content of your protein choices may be too high. Remember to stick to your daily protein requirement. Even though carbohydrates count more, caloric intake is still a factor during the weight loss phase.

11. Consider thyroid problems. If you suffer from low body temperature, cold hands and feet, dry skin, and brittle hair and nails, you may have hypothyroidism. Consult with your physician for a blood test to rule out the possibility of a thyroid problem.

12. Watch your consumption of low-carb products. Many low-carb products and chocolates sweetened with sugar alcohols have zero net carbs, but they still contain calories. Overconsumption of many of these products can lead to slowed weight loss. Exercise moderation in their consumption.

Creating Your Own Customized Menu Options

Creating your own menu options is easy. Just use your protein and carbohydrate food unit lists and the protein and carbohydrate allotment for each meal. The amount can be found on your Total Health menu according to your body frame size.

Let's take breakfast for a small body frame, for example.

BREAKFAST

21 grams of protein
10 grams of carbohydrates

On the protein food unit list, (pages 82–84), you'll see that 7 grams of protein equals one unit. In this example, you're allowed 21 grams of protein. Let's say you choose cottage cheese as your protein. How much can you have? If ¼ cup equals 7 grams of protein, you can have three units, or ¾ cup, of cottage cheese.

On the carbohydrate food unit list, (pages 84–85) you'll see that 9 grams of carbohydrates equals one unit. In this example, you're allowed 10 grams of carbohydrates. Let's say you choose pineapple as your carbohydrate. How much can you have? If ½ cup of pineapple equals 9 grams of carbohydrate, you can have one unit, or ½ cup, of pineapple.

You can create the same formula to create your own lunch, dinner, and snack options. Simply choose your favorite protein entrées and carbohydrates, staying within the limits of 21 grams of protein and 10 grams of carbohydrates or less at each meal.

Your Total Health program offers an infinite variety of protein and carbohydrate combinations. Check out the recipes in the Total Health recipe section of this book or the more than 120 recipes at www.totalhealthdoc.com and see for yourself. We also add new recipes every month. However, during your first couple of weeks on the program, for your convenience, we recommend that you follow the options on your Total Health menu.

Total Health Journal

Logging or journaling your menu options is another key to success on the Total Health plan. This allows you to stay accountable to yourself on a daily basis. It lets you look back at what choices you've been making and periodically evaluate your progress. This is also the same log I use with my patients in my private practice in Thousand Oaks, California.

Feel free to make copies of the Total Health Food Journal page below for your personal use in logging your Total Health meal menu options.

How to Use Your Food Journal Successfully

Dating Your Journal
Row 1, box 1: Write in the month.
Row 1, boxes 2–8: Write in the day and date.

Food Journaling: Be as detailed as possible. Be honest! This tool will serve you best when it brings to light your victories, as well as your weaknesses.

Vitamins: Check off the appropriate box for A.M. or P.M., depending on when you take your vitamins.

Water: Mark a box for each glass of water you drink. Remember to drink at least eight glasses a day.

Renewing your mind: Spend time each day taking care of your mental health. Some examples would be Continuing Education, Pursuing a Passion, Creative Outlet, Reading. Refer to Part V, "Mental Health: Helpful Hints for Happiness," (page 143) for more tips on renewing your mind.

Exercise: Spend time each day strengthening your body. Write in the type of exercises completed and the amount of time spent.

P = Passive   Do-it-yourself stretching exercises
A = Aerobic   Continuous and rhythmic, 20–30 minutes, (3 times per week; for example, walking, biking, or swimming)
R = Resistance   Training with weights or resistance bands

Refer to Part IV, "Exercise: How to Get Started and Why," (page 113) for more detailed information on passive, aerobic, and resistance exercise.

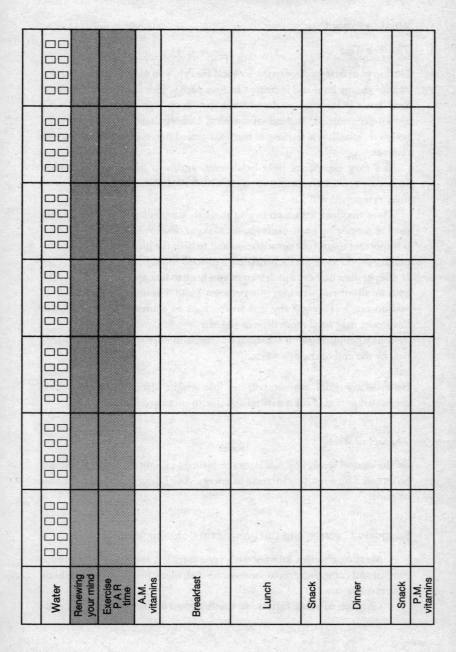

	Water	Renewing your mind	Exercise P.A.R. time	A.M. vitamins	Breakfast	Lunch	Snack	Dinner	Snack	P.M. vitamins
	☐☐ ☐☐ ☐☐ ☐☐									
	☐☐ ☐☐ ☐☐ ☐☐									
	☐☐ ☐☐ ☐☐ ☐☐									
	☐☐ ☐☐ ☐☐ ☐☐									
	☐☐ ☐☐ ☐☐ ☐☐									
	☐☐ ☐☐ ☐☐ ☐☐									
	☐☐ ☐☐ ☐☐ ☐☐									

What to Expect

The First Week

During your first week of living in Total Health, you may feel an initial dip in your energy level and increased hunger pangs. This is a natural reaction. Your body is learning to do without the cheap sugar rush to which it's grown accustomed. Instead of burning carbohydrates for energy, your body's metabolism is starting to burn the stored sugars in your liver and fat reserves.

You may experience light-headedness and/or a low-grade headache, which are typical symptoms of sugar withdrawal. After two to three days, these symptoms will pass.

More frequent urination is also natural. Your kidneys probably aren't used to processing up to eight glasses of water daily. Adequate water intake is important to prevent constipation and to help the kidneys eliminate natural by-products of the fat breakdown process through urine.

Depending on how much weight you have to lose and your daily carbohydrate allotment, you may lose between 2 and 5 pounds the first week. If you do not lose weight the first week, don't be alarmed. Your metabolic hormones may need more time to adjust.

Many people report a substantial increase in energy and mental sharpness by the end of the first week.

Note: Many times, women will not lose weight before and during their menstrual period. This is natural and due to increased fluid retention.

The Second Week

By the second week, any headaches or feelings of light-headedness should be replaced by a marked increase in energy. Any hunger pangs should also be gone.

Suggested Protein and Carbohydrate Combinations

• **Meat or chicken stir-fry** with vegetables is a tasty way to combine protein and carbohydrates in an easy one-dish meal. Flavor with teriyaki or your favorite sauce.

• **Chicken or steak fajitas** are another good option. You can add guacamole and sour cream as long as you count the guacamole as part of your carbohydrate allotment. Stay away from the chips and tortillas.

• **Chicken Caesar salad, Chinese chicken salad, and Cobb salad** are three other good combination choices, especially when dining out. Just be sure to ask for your salad dressing on the side, and don't overdo it.

• **Japanese cuisine:** Choose sashimi or chicken or steak teriyaki instead of sushi, which contains rice. Your may also have miso soup and cucumber or lettuce salad with your protein entrée.

• **Other Oriental cuisines:** Protein/carbohydrate combinations such as beef and broccoli, almond chicken, or shrimp and vegetables are good choices. Egg-drop or hot-and-sour soup are okay. Remember, use the ballpark technique (protein servings should be the size of your palm) to determine your portions, and stay away from the rice, noodles, and fortune cookies!

WHEN YOU REACH YOUR WEIGHT GOAL

Once you've reached your ideal body fat and weight, you can increase your carbohydrate intake to a one-to-one ratio of protein to carbohydrates to maintain your weight.

At this point you may also introduce some of the more "unfavorable" or "high-glycemic" types of carbohydrates back into your meal plan. These include rice, pasta, potatoes, etc.

Here's an example: Let's say you're a large body frame size and are allowed 28 grams of protein at each meal and 10 grams of carbohydrates in the form of fiber-rich fruits and vegetables during the weight loss phase. Now that you're at your target weight and are allowed a one-to-one ratio of protein to carbohydrates, you would be able to have about 28 grams of protein to 27 grams of carbohydrates. You could now consider allowing yourself to have a few of the "unfavorable" carbohydrate choices as part of your total carbohydrate allotment, as outlined in the following example.

• *Protein (28 grams):* **Chicken (4–6 ounces), beef (4–6 ounces), pork (4–6 ounces), fish (6 ounces),** or **your favorite protein.**

• *Carbohydrates (27 grams):* **Favorite vegetables** and/or **green salad:** Choose 3 units (27 carbohydrate grams) of your favorite vegetable. You may combine several different carbohydrate choices together as long as the total grams of carbohydrate add up to 3 units (27 grams). Example: ¼ cup of pasta or rice plus 1 cup of broccoli.

Caution: Don't fall back into the trap of eating too many "unfavorable" high-glycemic carbohydrates. We still want you to choose the "favorable" low-glycemic carbohydrates in the form of fiber-rich fruits and vegetables the majority of the time!

MACRONUTRIENT UNITS LISTS

The following protein and carbohydrate lists have been provided to help you when creating your customized meal plans. Simply choose your favorite protein and carbohydrate choices. Remember to make your protein choices from the "Best Choice," categories whenever possible. These are the proteins that are lower in fat content.

All of the vegetables and fruits in the "Carbohydrate Choices" section have a low glycemic index. This means that they don't cause a rapid rise in blood sugar levels.

Macronutrient Units
Protein Choices
(APPROXIMATELY 7 GRAMS OF PROTEIN PER UNIT)

Meat and Poultry

Best Choices

Chicken breast, deli-style,
   1.5 ounces
Chicken breast, skinless
   1.0 ounce
Turkey breast, deli-style,
   1.5 ounces
Turkey breast, skinless, 1.0 ounce
Veal, 1.0 ounce

Fair Choices

Beef, ground (10%–15%),
   1.5 ounces

Beef, jerky, 1.0 ounce
Beef, lean cuts, 1.0 ounce
Canadian bacon, lean,
   1.0 ounce
Chicken, dark meat, skinless,
   1.0 ounce
Corned beef, lean, 1.0 ounce
Duck, 1.5 ounces
Ham, deli-style, 1.5 ounces
Ham, lean, 1.0 ounce
Lamb, lean, 1.0 ounce
Pork chop, 1.0 ounce
Pork, lean, 1.0 ounce
Turkey bacon, 3 strips
Turkey burger, 1.0 ounce

Meat and Poultry (cont.)

Turkey, dark meat, skinless,
    1.0 ounce
Turkey jerky, 1.0 ounce
Turkey sausage, 1.0 ounce

Poor Choices

Bacon, 3 strips
Beef, fatty cuts, 1.0 ounce
Beef, ground (more than 15%),
    1.5 ounces
Hot dog (chicken or turkey),
    1 link
Hot dog (pork or beef), 1 link
Kielbasa, 2.0 ounces
Liver, beef, 1.0 ounce
Liver, chicken, 1.0 ounce
Pepperoni, 1.0 ounce
Pork sausage, 2 links
Salami, 1.0 ounce

Protein-Rich Dairy Products

Best Choices

Cheese, fat-free, 1.0 ounce
Cottage cheese, low fat, ¼ cup
Cottage cheese, nonfat, ¼ cup

Fair Choices

Cheese, reduced fat, 1.0 ounce
Cream cheese, reduced fat,
    3.0 ounces
Mozzarella cheese, skim,
    1.0 ounce
Ricotta cheese, skim, 2.0 ounces

Poor Choices

Hard cheese, 1.0 ounce

Fish and Seafood

Best Choices

Bass, 1.5 ounces
Bluefish, 1.5 ounces
Calamari, 1.5 ounces
Catfish, 1.5 ounces
Clams, 1.5 ounces
Cod, 1.5 ounces
Crabmeat, 1.5 ounces
Haddock, 1.5 ounces
Halibut, 1.5 ounces
Lobster, 1.5 ounces
Mackerel, 1.5 ounces
Salmon, 1.5 ounces
Sardines, 1.5 ounces
Scallops, 1.5 ounces
Shrimp, 1.5 ounces
Snapper, 1.5 ounces
Swordfish, 1.5 ounces
Trout, 1.5 ounces
Tuna, 1.5 ounces
Tuna, canned in water, 1.0 ounce

Eggs

Best Choices

Egg substitute, ¼ cup
Egg whites, 2

Poor Choices

Whole egg, 1

Vegetarian

Best Choices

Protein powder, ⅓ ounce
Soy burger, ½ patty
Soy hot dog, 1 link
Soy sausages, 2 links

Vegetarian (cont.)
Tofu, firm or extra firm,
   1.0 ounce
Tofu, soft, 3.0 ounces

Mixed Protein–Carbohydrate Foods (contains one unit of protein = 7 grams and one unit of carbohydrate = 9 grams)

Almond butter (natural),
   2 tablespoons

Milk (1%), 1 cup
Nuts (any type), 1 ounce
Peanut butter (natural),
   2 tablespoons
Yogurt, plain, ½ cup

Macronutrient Units
Carbohydrate Choices
(APPROXIMATELY 9 GRAMS OF CARBOHYDRATE PER UNIT)

Vegetables

Cooked Vegetables

Artichoke, 1 small
Asparagus, 1 cup (12 spears)
Beans, black (canned), ⅓ cup
Beans, green or wax, 1 cup
Broccoli, 1 cup
Brussels sprouts, 1 cup
Cabbage, 1½ cups
Cauliflower, 1½ cups
Chickpeas, 1 cup
Collard greens, 1 cup
Eggplant, 1½ cups
Kale, 1 cup
Kidney beans (canned), 1 cup
Leeks (sliced), ⅓ cup
Lentils, ⅓ cup
Mushrooms, 1 cup
Okra (sliced), 1 cup
Onions (boiled), 1 cup
Sauerkraut, 1 cup

Swiss chard, 1 cup
Turnip (mashed), 1 cup
Turnip greens, 1½ cups
Yellow squash, 1 cup
Zucchini, 1 cup

Raw Vegetables

Alfalfa sprouts, ½ cup
Avocados (California), 1 medium
Bean sprouts, 3 cups
Broccoli, 2 cups
Cabbage (shredded), 2 cups
Cauliflower, 2 cups
Celery, 2 cups (sliced) or 4 stalks
Cucumber, 1
Cucumber (sliced), 3 cups
Endive (chopped), 5 cups
Escarole (chopped), 5 cups
Green pepper (chopped), 1½ cups
Green peppers, 2
Hummus, ⅓ cup
Lettuce, iceberg (1 head)

Vegetables (cont.)

Lettuce, romaine (chopped),
    6 cups
Mushrooms (chopped), 3 cups
Onion (chopped), 1 cup
Radishes (sliced), 2 cups
Salsa, ½ cup
Snow peas, 1 cup
Spinach, 4 cups
Spinach salad (2 cups raw
    spinach, ¼ cup raw onion,
    ½ cup raw mushrooms, and
    ¼ cup raw tomatoes)
Tomato (chopped), 1 cup
Tomatoes, 2
Tossed salad (2 cups shredded
    lettuce, ½ cup raw green
    pepper, ½ cup raw cucumber,
    and ½ cup raw tomato)
Water chestnuts, ½ cup

Fruit (Fresh, Frozen, or Canned)

Apple, ½
Applesauce, ⅓ cup
Apricots, 3
Blackberries, ½ cup
Blueberries, ½ cup
Cantaloupe, ¼
Cherries, 7
Fruit cocktail (in light syrup),
    ½ cup

Grapefruit, ½
Grapes, ½ cup
Honeydew melon (cubed), ½ cup
Kiwi, 1
Lemon, 1
Lime, 1
Mandarin orange (in light syrup),
    ⅓ cup
Nectarine, ½
Orange, ½
Peach, 1
Peaches (in light syrup), ½ cup
Pear, ⅓
Pineapple (cubed), ½ cup
Plum, 1
Raspberries, ⅔ cup
Strawberries, 1 cup
Tangerine, 1
Watermelon (cubed), ½ cup

Grains and Breads

Bagel, ⅓
Bread, ½ slice
English muffin, ½
Hamburger bun, ½
Oatmeal (slow-cooking), ⅓ cup
    (cooked) or ½ ounce (dry)
Pasta, ¼ cup
Rice, ¼ cup
Tortilla, corn (6-inch), 1
Tortilla, flour (8-inch), ½

TOTAL HEALTH PROTEIN-RICH, FAVORABLE-CARBOHYDRATE MENU OPTIONS

Petite Body Frame
(60–70 Grams of Protein per Day)

MODERATE WEIGHT LOSS
(40 Grams of Carbohydrates per Day)

BREAKFAST (8:00 A.M.)
14 grams protein
10 grams carbohydrate

OPTION 1

Protein
½ cup low-fat (2%) or nonfat cottage cheese

Carbohydrate
Favorite fruit: Choose 1 unit (9 carbohydrate grams) of your favorite fruit listed on the "Macronutrient Units" list (page 85).

OPTION 2

Protein
Omelette (made with 2 egg whites or ¼ cup of egg substitute) with **1 ounce cheese *or* 1 ounce meat.** (If you do not want meat, substitute an extra egg white, ¼ cup of egg substitute, or 1 ounce cheese.) You may add carbohydrates from the "Macronutrient Units" list (page 84), such as mushrooms, onions, salsa, and avocados, but be sure to count them as part of your total carbohydrate intake.

Carbohydrate
Favorite fruit: Choose 1 unit (9 grams carbohydrate) of your favorite fruit or other carbohydrate listed on the "Macronutrient Units" list (page 84). Examples: ½ apple, 1 tomato, ⅓ bagel, ½ English muffin, 1 low-carbohydrate tortilla, 1 slice of toast (low-carbohydrate bread).

OPTION 3

Protein
Choose one of the following: 2 cheese sticks (string cheese), **2 ounces cheese** (reduced fat), **2 ounces lean deli meat,** *or* **2 ounces turkey jerky** (low sodium).

Carbohydrate
Favorite fruit: Choose 1 unit (9 carbohydrate grams) of your favorite fruit listed on the "Macronutrient Units" list (page 85).

OPTION 4

Protein
Choose one of the following: 1 cheese stick (string cheese), **1 ounce cheese** (reduced fat), **1 ounce lean deli meat,** *or* **1 ounce turkey jerky** (low sodium).

Carbohydrate and Protein
½ 40-30-30 protein bar *or* **1 protein bar, do not add cheese if the protein to carbohydrate ratio is adequate (14 grams of protein to 10 grams or less of carbohydrates).**

OPTION 5

Protein
Choose one of the following: 2 cheese sticks (string cheese), **2 ounces cheese** (reduced fat), **2 ounces lean deli meat, 2 ounces turkey jerky** (low sodium), *or* **1 scoop protein powder (14 grams of protein) to mix into yogurt.**

Carbohydrate and Protein
¼ cup light yogurt (any flavor) **or ½ cup plain yogurt**

OPTION 6 (FAST-FOOD OPTION)

Breakfast sandwich: 1 egg and cheese or meat (without top muffin or bun)
Breakfast burrito: 1 egg and cheese burrito (tear off ½ tortilla)

OPTION 7

Choose one of the following: ⅓ bagel, ½ English muffin, 1 low-carbohydrate tortilla, *or* 1 slice toast (low-carbohydrate bread) **with one of the following: 2 ounces cream cheese and/or lox (smoked salmon), 1 tablespoon natural peanut or other nut butter with 1 cheese stick, 1 ounce cheese** (reduced fat), *or* **1 ounce lean deli meat.**

OPTION 8

⅓ cup oatmeal with 1 scoop protein powder or omelette (made with 2 egg whites or ¼ cup egg substitute)

OPTION 9

1 protein meal replacement bar or shake (14 grams of protein to 10 grams or less of carbohydrates). If you're making your own meal replacement shake with protein powder, add it to milk or water. Remember that 8 ounces of milk contain about 7 grams of protein and 9 grams of carbohydrates. Therefore you'll need to account for the protein and carbohydrates in the milk.

LUNCH (NOON) AND DINNER (7:00 P.M.)
14 grams protein
10 grams carbohydrate

OPTION 1

Protein
Chicken (2–3 ounces), beef (2–3 ounces), pork (2–3 ounces), fish (3–4 ounces), *or* your favorite protein choice from the "Macronutrient Units" list (page 82). You may add approximately 1 tablespoon of your favorite sauce (barbecue, teriyaki, etc.) and your favorite spices.

Carbohydrate
Favorite vegetables *and/or* green salad: Choose 1 unit (9 carbohydrate grams) of your favorite vegetable listed on the "Macronutrient Units" list (page 84). You may combine several different vegetables as long as the total

grams of carbohydrate add up to 1 unit (9 grams). Example: 1 cup of cauliflower and ½ cup of broccoli.

See "Food Preparation Tips" (page 67) for butter and salad dressing recommendations.

OPTION 2

Protein
Tuna (2–3 ounces), chicken (2–3 ounces), *or* egg salad (2–3 ounces) (with reduced-fat mayonnaise), *or* lean deli meat (2–3 ounces). You may also add cheese, lettuce, tomato, onion, pickles, or your favorite garnishes as long as you account for their protein and carbohydrate content.

Carbohydrate
Choose one of the following: 1 small tossed lettuce salad, 1 tomato, 1 medium-size avocado, ⅓ bagel, ½ English muffin, 1 low-carbohydrate tortilla, or 1 slice low-carbohydrate bread. You may add mayonnaise and mustard to taste.

OPTION 3 (FAST-FOOD OPTIONS)

Garden fresh salads: 1 salad with your favorite protein choice (with your favorite dressing, no croutons)
Chicken or steak burrito: 1 burrito (no tortilla or ½ tortilla without rice and beans). Guacamole, salsa, and sour cream are fine in conservative amounts.
Chicken or steak soft taco: 1 soft taco (tear off ½ tortilla)
Deli-style or sub sandwich: 1 sandwich with your choice of meat or cheese (without top bun or protein style—wrapped in lettuce)
Grilled chicken sandwich: 1 grilled chicken sandwich (without top bun or protein style—wrapped in lettuce)
Rotisserie or grilled chicken: 1 skinless thigh, leg, or breast with 1 side coleslaw
Hamburger: ¼ pound hamburger or cheeseburger (without top bun or protein style—wrapped in lettuce)
Pizza: 2 slices (don't eat the crust, eat only the toppings: cheese, lean meats)

You will maintain a low-fat diet naturally by making your protein choices from the "Best Choice" categories in the Macronutrient Units list (page 82).

SNACK (3:30 AND OPTIONALLY 11:00 P.M.)
7 grams protein
5 grams carbohydrate

OPTION 1

1 celery stalk filled with 1 tablespoon of natural peanut or other nut butter *or* 2 ounces cream cheese (reduced fat)

OPTION 2

Choose one of the following: 1 cheese stick (string cheese), **1 ounce cheese** (reduced fat), or **1 ounce lean deli meat** with your **favorite fruit**—choose ½ unit (4.5 carbohydrate grams of your **favorite fruit** from the "Macronutrient Units" list (page 85).

OPTION 3

¼ cup nuts (any type)

OPTION 4

1 (6- to 8-ounce) hot or iced caffelatte (1% or 2% milk) **coffee drink** (sugar-free). Ask the coffee establishment to add a shot of flavored sugar-free syrup if available. You may also ask to blend your iced caffelatte in the blender with sugar-free syrup added for a sugar-free ice blended coffee drink. Some coffee establishments have preprepared sugar-free ice blended coffee drinks.

OPTION 5

1 (4- to 6-ounce) glass of milk (skim, 1%, or 2%)

OPTION 6

½ **cup light yogurt** (any flavor) *or* ½ **cup plain yogurt** (you may add your favorite sugar-free syrup flavor). You may also choose a low-carb yogurt/ dairy snack option (approximately 7 grams of protein to 5 grams of carbohydrates).

OPTION 7

½ **40-30-30** *or* **protein bar** (approximately 7 grams of protein to 5 grams of carbohydrates)

OPTION 8

Choose one of the following: 1 (4- to 6-ounce) glass of wine (dry red or dry white) *or* **1 light beer with one of the following: 1 cheese stick** (string cheese), **1 ounce cheese** (reduced fat), **1 ounce lean deli meat,** *or* **1 ounce turkey jerky** (low sodium).

OPTION 9

1 deviled *or* **hard-cooked egg**

OPTION 10

¼ **cup ice cream** (any brand or flavor) **with 1 ounce cheese** (reduced fat) *or* ¼ **cup low-carb ice cream without cheese** (approximately 7 grams of protein to 5 grams of carbohydrates)

"FREE" SNACKS:

Sugar-free Jell-O and homemade sugar-free Popsicles (made in a Popsicle mold with Crystal Light lemonade or sugar-free soda) are about the only acceptable *free* snacks. You may add some reduced-fat whipped cream to the Jell-O.

You may also eat some **low-carb, sugar-free chocolate bars** *or* **candies** with zero net carbs to satisfy your occasional sweet tooth, but not in unlimited amounts. They still contain calories, sugar alcohols, and fat.

Refer to Appendix B, "Recommended Products," for the best-tasting high-quality low-carb product brands available.

Small Body Frame
(70–80 Grams of Protein per Day)
MODERATE WEIGHT LOSS
(40 Grams of Carbohydrates per Day)

BREAKFAST (8:00 A.M.)
21 grams protein
10 grams carbohydrate

OPTION 1

Protein
¾ cup low-fat (2%) *or* nonfat cottage cheese

Carbohydrate
Favorite fruit: Choose 1 unit (9 carbohydrate grams) of your favorite fruit listed on the "Macronutrient Units" list (page 85).

OPTION 2

Protein
Omelette (made with 2 egg whites or ¼ cup of egg substitute) with **1 ounce cheese *and* 1 ounce meat.** (If you do not want meat, substitute an extra egg white, ¼ cup of egg substitute or 1 ounce cheese.) You may add carbohydrates from the "Macronutrient Units" list (page 84), such as mushrooms, onions, salsa, and avocados, but be sure to count them as part of your total carbohydrate intake.

Carbohydrate
Favorite fruit: Choose 1 unit (9 carbohydrate grams) of your favorite fruit or other carbohydrate listed on the "Macronutrient Units" list (page 85). Examples: ½ apple, 1 tomato, ⅓ bagel, ½ English muffin, 1 low-carbohydrate tortilla, 1 slice of toast (low-carbohydrate bread).

OPTION 3

Protein

Choose one of the following: 3 cheese sticks (string cheese), **3 ounces cheese** (reduced fat), **3 ounces lean deli meat,** *or* **3 ounces turkey jerky** (low sodium)

Carbohydrate

Favorite fruit: Choose 1 unit (9 carbohydrate grams) of your favorite fruit listed on the Macronutrient Units list (page 85).

OPTION 4

Protein

Choose one of the following: 2 cheese sticks (string cheese), **2 ounces cheese** (reduced fat), **2 ounces lean deli meat,** *or* **2 ounces turkey jerky** (low sodium).

Carbohydrate and Protein

½ 40-30-30 protein bar *or* **1 protein bar, do not add cheese if the protein to carbohydrate ratio is adequate (21 grams of protein to 10 grams or less of carbohydrates).**

OPTION 5

Protein

Choose one of the following: 3 cheese sticks (string cheese), **3 ounces cheese** (reduced fat), **3 ounces lean deli meat, 3 ounces turkey jerky** (low sodium), *or* **1½ scoops protein powder (21 grams of protein) to mix into yogurt.**

Carbohydrate and Protein

¼ cup light yogurt (any flavor) *or* **½ cup plain yogurt**

OPTION 6 (FAST-FOOD OPTION)

Breakfast sandwich: 1 egg, cheese, and meat (without top muffin or bun)

Breakfast burrito: 1 egg and cheese burrito (tear off ½ tortilla)

OPTION 7

Choose one of the following: ⅓ bagel, ½ English muffin, 1 low-carbohydrate tortilla, *or* 1 slice toast (low-carbohydrate bread) **with one of the following: 3 ounces cream cheese and/or lox** (smoked salmon), **1 tablespoon natural peanut or other nut butter with 1 cheese stick, 2 ounces cheese** (reduced fat), *or* **2 ounces lean deli meat.**

OPTION 8

⅓ cup oatmeal with 1 scoop protein powder *or* omelette (made with 2 egg whites *or* ¼ cup egg substitute)

OPTION 9

1 protein meal replacement bar or shake (21 grams of protein to 10 grams or less of carbohydrates). If you're making your own meal replacement shake with protein powder, add it to milk or water. Remember that 8 ounces of milk contain about 7 grams of protein and 9 grams of carbohydrates. Therefore you'll need to account for the protein and carbohydrates in the milk.

LUNCH (NOON) AND DINNER (7:00 P.M.)
21 grams protein
10 grams carbohydrate

OPTION 1

Protein
Chicken (3–4 ounces), beef (3–4 ounces), pork (3–4 ounces), fish (4.5 ounces), *or* your favorite protein choice from the "Macronutrient Units" list (pages 82–84). You may add approximately 1 tablespoon of your favorite sauce (barbecue, teriyaki, etc.) and your favorite spices.

Carbohydrate
Favorite vegetables *and/or* green salad: Choose 1 unit (9 carbohydrate grams) of your favorite vegetable choices listed on the "Macronutrient Units" list (pages 84–85). You may combine several different vegetables as

long as the total grams of carbohydrate add up to 1 unit (9 grams). Example: 1 cup of cauliflower and ½ cup of broccoli.

See "Food Preparation Tips" (page 67) for butter and salad dressing recommendations.

OPTION 2

Protein
Tuna (3–4 ounces), chicken (3–4 ounces), *or* egg salad (3–4 ounces) (with reduced-fat mayonnaise) *or* lean deli meat (3–4 ounces). You may also add cheese, lettuce, tomato, onion, pickles, or your favorite garnishes as long as you account for their protein and carbohydrate content.

Carbohydrate
Choose one of the following: 1 small tossed lettuce salad, 1 tomato, 1 medium-size avocado, ⅓ bagel, ½ English muffin, 1 low-carbohydrate tortilla, *or* 1 slice low-carbohydrate bread. You may add mayonnaise and mustard to taste.

OPTION 3 (FAST-FOOD OPTIONS)

Garden fresh salad: 1 salad with your favorite protein choice (with your favorite dressing, no croutons)
Chicken or steak burrito: 1 burrito (no tortilla or ½ tortilla without rice and beans). Guacamole, salsa, and sour cream are fine in conservative amounts.
Chicken or steak soft taco: 1 soft taco (tear off ½ tortilla)
Deli-style or sub sandwich: 1 sandwich with your choice of meat or cheese (without top bun or protein style—wrapped in lettuce)
Grilled chicken sandwich: 1 grilled chicken sandwich (without top bun or protein style—wrapped in lettuce)
Rotisserie or grilled chicken: 1 skinless thigh, leg, or breast with 1 side coleslaw
Hamburger: ¼ pound hamburger or cheeseburger (without top bun or protein style—wrapped in lettuce)
Pizza: 2 slices (don't eat the crust, eat only the toppings:—cheese, lean meats)

You will maintain a low-fat diet naturally by making your protein choices from the "Best Choice" categories on the "Macronutrient Units" list (page 82).

SNACK (3:30 AND OPTIONALLY 11:00 P.M.)
7 grams protein
5 grams carbohydrate

OPTION 1

1 celery stalk filled with 1 tablespoon of natural peanut or other nut butter *or* 2 ounces of cream cheese (reduced fat)

OPTION 2

Choose one of the following: 1 cheese stick (string cheese), **1 ounce, cheese** (reduced fat), *or* **1 ounce lean deli meat** with your **favorite fruit**—choose ½ unit (4.5 carbohydrate grams) of your favorite fruit from the "Macronutrient Units list (page 85).

OPTION 3

¼ cup nuts (any type)

OPTION 4

1 6- to 8-ounce hot or iced caffelatte (1% or 2% milk) **coffee drink** (sugar-free). Ask the coffee establishment to add a shot of flavored sugar-free syrup if available. You may also ask to blend your iced caffelatte in the blender with sugar-free syrup added for a sugar-free ice blended coffee drink. Some coffee establishments have prepared sugar-free ice blended coffee drinks.

OPTION 5

1 (4- to 6-ounce) glass of milk (skim, 1%, or 2%)

OPTION 6

½ cup light yogurt (any flavor) *or* **½ cup plain yogurt** (you may add your favorite sugar-free syrup flavor). You may also choose a low-carb yogurt/

dairy snack option (approximately 7 grams of protein to 5 grams of carbo-hydrates).

OPTION 7

½ 40-30-30 *or* protein bar (approximately 7 grams of protein to 5 grams of carbohydrates)

OPTION 8

Choose one of the following: 1 (4- to 6-ounce) glass of wine (dry red or dry white) *or* 1 light beer with one of the following: 1 cheese stick (string cheese), 1 ounce cheese (reduced fat), 1 ounce lean deli meat, *or* 1 ounce turkey jerky (low sodium).

OPTION 9

1 deviled or hard-cooked egg

OPTION 10

¼ cup ice cream (any brand or flavor) with 1 ounce cheese (reduced fat) *or* ¼ cup low-carb ice cream without cheese (approximately 7 grams of protein to 5 grams of carbohydrates)

"FREE" SNACKS

Sugar-free Jell-O and homemade sugar-free Popsicles (made in a Popsicle mold with Crystal Light lemonade or sugar-free soda) are about the only acceptable *free* snacks. You may add some reduced-fat whipped cream to the Jell-O.

You may also eat some low-carb, sugar-free chocolate bars *or* candies with zero net carbs to satisfy your occasional sweet tooth, but not in un-limited amounts. They still contain calories, sugar alcohols, and fat.

Refer to Appendix B, "Recommended Products," for the best-tasting high-quality low-carb product brands available.

Medium Body Frame
(70–80 Grams of Protein per Day)
MODERATE WEIGHT LOSS
(40 grams of Carbohydrates per Day)

BREAKFAST (8:00 A.M.)
21 grams protein
10 grams carbohydrate

OPTION 1

Protein
¾ cup of low-fat (2%) *or* nonfat cottage cheese

Carbohydrate
Favorite fruit: Choose 1 unit (9 carbohydrate grams) of your favorite fruit listed on the "Macronutrient Units" list (page 85).

OPTION 2

Protein
Omelette (made with 2 egg whites or ¼ cup of egg substitute) **with 1 ounce cheese *and* 1 ounce meat** (if you do not want meat, substitute an extra egg white, ¼ cup of egg substitute, or 1 ounce cheese). You may add carbohydrates from the "Macronutrient Units" list (page 84), such as mushrooms, onions, salsa, and avocados, but be sure to count them as part of your total carbohydrate intake.

Carbohydrate
Favorite fruit: Choose 1 unit (9 carbohydrate grams) of your favorite fruit or other carbohydrate listed on the "Macronutrient Units" list (page 85). Examples: ½ apple, 1 tomato, ⅓ bagel, ½ English muffin, 1 low-carbohydrate tortilla, 1 slice of toast (low-carbohydrate bread).

OPTION 3

Protein
Choose one of the following: 3 cheese sticks (string cheese), **3 ounces cheese** (reduced fat), **3 ounces lean deli meat, *or* turkey jerky** (low sodium).

Carbohydrate
Favorite fruit: Choose 1 unit (9 carbohydrate grams) of your favorite fruit listed on the "Macronutrient Units" list (page 85).

OPTION 4

Protein
Choose one of the following: 2 cheese sticks (string cheese), **2 ounces cheese** (reduced fat), **2 ounce lean deli meat,** *or* **2 ounces turkey jerky** (low sodium).

Carbohydrate and Protein
½ 40-30-30 protein bar *or* **1 protein bar, do not add cheese if the protein to carbohydrate ratio is adequate (14 grams of protein to 10 grams or less of carbohydrates).**

OPTION 5

Protein
Choose one of the following: 3 cheese sticks (string cheese), **3 ounces cheese** (reduced fat), **3 ounces lean deli meat, 3 ounces turkey jerky** (low sodium), *or* **1½ scoops protein powder (21 grams of protein) to mix into yogurt.**

Carbohydrate and Protein
¼ cup light yogurt (any flavor) *or* **½ cup plain yogurt**

OPTION 6 (FAST-FOOD OPTION)

Breakfast sandwich: 1 egg, cheese, and meat (without top muffin or bun)
Breakfast burrito: 1 egg and cheese burrito (tear off ½ tortilla)

OPTION 7

Choose one of the following: ⅓ bagel, ½ English muffin, 1 low-carbohydrate tortilla, *or* **1 slice toast** (low-carbohydrate bread) **with one of the following: 3 ounces cream cheese and/or lox** (smoked salmon), **1 tablespoon natural peanut or other nut butter with 1 cheese stick, 2 ounces cheese** (reduced fat), *or* **2 ounces lean deli meat.**

OPTION 8

⅓ **cup oatmeal with 1 scoop protein powder** *or* **omelette** (made with 2 egg whites or ¼ cup egg substitute)

OPTION 9

1 protein meal replacement bar *or* **shake** (21 grams of protein to 10 grams or less of carbohydrates). If you're making your own meal replacement shake with protein powder, add it to milk or water. Remember that 8 ounces of milk contain about 7 grams of protein and 9 grams of carbohydrates. Therefore you'll need to account for the protein and carbohydrates in the milk.

LUNCH (NOON) AND DINNER (7:00 P.M.)
21 grams protein
10 grams carbohydrate

OPTION 1

Protein
Chicken (3–4 ounces), beef (3–4 ounces), pork, (3–4 ounces) fish (4.5 ounces), *or* **your favorite protein choice** from the "Macronutrient Units" list (page 82). You may add approximately 1 tablespoon of your favorite sauce (barbecue, teriyaki, etc.) and your favorite spices.

Carbohydrate
Favorite vegetables *and/or* **green salad:** Choose 1 unit (9 carbohydrate grams) of your favorite vegetable listed on the "Macronutrient Units" list (page 84). You may combine several different vegetables as long as the total grams of carbohydrate add up to 1 unit (9 grams). Example: 1 cup of cauliflower and ½ cup of broccoli.

See "Food Preparation Tips" (page 67) for butter and salad dressing recommendations.

OPTION 2

Protein
Tuna (3–4 ounces), chicken (3–4 ounces), *or* **egg salad (3–4 ounces)** (with reduced-fat mayonnaise) *or* **lean deli meat (3–4 ounces).** You may

also add cheese, lettuce, tomato, onion, pickles, or your favorite garnishes as long as you account for their protein and carbohydrate content.

Carbohydrate
Choose one of the following: 1 small tossed lettuce salad, 1 tomato, 1 medium-size avocado, ⅓ bagel, ½ English muffin, 1 low-carbohydrate tortilla or 1 slice bread (low carbohydrate). You may add mayonnaise and mustard to taste.

OPTION 3 (FAST-FOOD OPTIONS)

Garden fresh salad: 1 salad with your favorite protein choice (with your favorite dressing, no croutons)
Chicken *or* steak burrito: 1 burrito (no tortilla or ½ tortilla without rice and beans). Guacamole, salsa, and sour cream are fine in conservative amounts.
Chicken *or* steak soft taco: 1 soft taco (tear off ½ tortilla)
Deli-style *or* sub sandwich: 1 sandwich with your choice of meat or cheese (without top bun or protein style—wrapped in lettuce)
Grilled chicken sandwich: 1 grilled chicken sandwich (without top bun or protein style—wrapped in lettuce)
Rotisserie or grilled chicken: 1 skinless thigh, leg, or breast with 1 side coleslaw
Hamburger: ¼ pound hamburger or cheeseburger (without top bun or protein style—wrapped in lettuce)
Pizza: 2 slices (don't eat the crust, eat only the toppings: cheese, lean meats)

You will maintain a low-fat diet naturally by making your protein choices from the "Best Choices" categories appearing in the "Macronutrient Units" list (page 82).

SNACK (3:30 AND OPTIONALLY 11:00 P.M.)
7 grams protein
5 grams carbohydrate

OPTION 1

1 celery stalk filled with 1 tablespoon of natural peanut or nut butter *or* 2 ounces cream cheese (reduced fat)

OPTION 2

Choose one of the following: 1 cheese stick (string cheese), **1 ounce cheese** (reduced fat), *or* **1 ounce lean deli meat** with your **favorite fruit**—choose ½ unit (4.5 carbohydrate grams) of your favorite fruit from the "Macronutrient Units" list (page 85).

OPTION 3

¼ cup nuts (any type)

OPTION 4

1 (6- to 8-ounce) hot or iced caffelatte (1% or 2% milk) **coffee drink** (sugar-free). Ask the coffee establishment to add a shot of flavored sugar-free syrup if available. You may also ask to blend your iced caffelatte in the blender with sugar-free syrup added for a sugar-free ice blended coffee drink. Some coffee establishments have prepared sugar-free ice blended coffee drinks.

OPTION 5

1 (4- to 6-ounce) glass of milk (skim, 1%, or 2%)

OPTION 6

½ cup light yogurt (any flavor) or **½ cup plain yogurt** (you may add your favorite sugar-free syrup flavor). You may also choose a low-carb yogurt/ dairy snack option (approximately 7 grams of protein to 5 grams of carbohydrates).

OPTION 7

½ 40-30-30 *or* **protein bar** (approximately 7 grams of protein to 5 grams of carbohydrates)

OPTION 8

Choose one of the following: 1 (4- to 6-ounce) glass of wine (dry red or dry white) *or* **1 light beer** with one of the following: **1 cheese stick** (string cheese), **1 ounce cheese** (reduced fat), **1 ounce lean deli meat,** *or* **1 ounce turkey jerky** (low sodium).

OPTION 9

1 deviled or hard-cooked egg

OPTION 10

¼ **cup ice cream** (any brand or flavor) **with 1 ounce cheese** (reduced fat) *or* ¼ **cup low-carb ice cream without cheese** (approximately 7 grams of protein to 5 grams of carbohydrates)

"FREE" SNACKS

Sugar-free Jell-O and homemade sugar-free Popsicles (made in a Popsicle mold with Crystal Light lemonade or sugar-free soda) are about the only acceptable *free* snacks. You may also add some reduced-fat whipped cream to the Jell-O.

You may also eat some **low-carb, sugar-free chocolate bars** *or* **candies** with zero net carbs to satisfy your occasional sweet tooth, but not in unlimited amounts. They still contain calories, sugar alcohols, and fat.

Refer to Appendix B, "Recommended Products," for the best-tasting high-quality low-carb product brands available.

Large Body Frame
(90–100 grams of Protein per Day)
MODERATE WEIGHT LOSS
(40 Grams of Carbohydrates per Day)

BREAKFAST (8:00 A.M.)
28 grams protein
10 grams carbohydrate

OPTION 1

Protein
1 cup of low-fat (2%) *or* **nonfat cottage cheese**

Carbohydrate
Favorite fruit: Choose 1 unit (9 carbohydrate grams) of your favorite fruit listed on the "Macronutrient Units" list (page 85).

OPTION 2

Protein

Omelette (made with 2–3 egg whites or ½ cup of egg substitute) with **1–2 ounces cheese** *and* **1 ounce meat**. (If you do not want meat, substitute an extra egg white, ¼ cup of egg substitute, or 1 ounce cheese.) You may add carbohydrates from the "Macronutrient Units" list (page 84), such as mushrooms, onions, salsa, and avocados, but be sure to count them as part of your total carbohydrate intake.

Carbohydrate

Favorite fruit: Choose 1 unit (9 carbohydrate grams) of your favorite fruit or other carbohydrate listed on the "Macronutrient Units" list (page 85). Examples: ½ apple, 1 tomato, ⅓ bagel, ½ English muffin, 1 low-carbohydrate tortilla, 1 slice of toast (low-carbohydrate bread).

OPTION 3

Protein

Choose one of the following: 4 cheese sticks (string cheese), **4 ounces cheese** (reduced fat), **4 ounces lean deli meat,** *or* **4 ounces turkey jerky** (low sodium).

Carbohydrate

Favorite fruit: Choose 1 unit (9 carbohydrate grams) of your favorite fruit listed on the "Macronutrient Units" list (page 85).

OPTION 4

Protein

Choose one of the following: 3 cheese sticks (string cheese), **3 ounces cheese** (reduced fat) **3 ounces lean deli meat,** *or* **3 ounces turkey jerky** (low sodium).

Carbohydrate and Protein

½ 40-30-30 protein bar *or* **1 protein bar; do not add cheese if the protein to carbohydrate ratio is adequate** (28 grams of protein to 10 grams or less of carbohydrates).

OPTION 5

Protein
Choose one of the following: 3 cheese sticks (string cheese), **3 ounces cheese** (reduced fat), **2 ounces lean deli meat, 3 ounces turkey jerky** (low sodium), *or* **2 scoops Protein Powder** (28 grams of protein) **to mix into yogurt.**

Carbohydrate and Protein
¼ **cup light yogurt** (any flavor) *or* ½ **cup plain yogurt**

OPTION 6 (FAST-FOOD OPTION)

Breakfast sandwich: 2 eggs, cheese, and meat (without top muffin or bun)
Breakfast burrito: 2 egg and cheese burritos (tear off ½ tortilla)

OPTION 7

Choose one of the following: ⅓ **bagel,** ½ **English muffin, 1 low-carbohydrate tortilla,** *or* **1 slice toast** (low-carbohydrate brand) **with one of the following: 4 ounces cream cheese and/or lox** (smoked salmon), **1 tablespoon natural peanut or other nut butter with 1 cheese stick, 3 ounces cheese** (reduced fat), *or* **3 ounces lean deli meat.**

OPTION 8

⅓ **cup oatmeal with 2 scoops protein powder or omelette** (made with 2 egg whites or ¼ cup egg substitute)

OPTION 9

1 protein meal replacement bar or shake (28 grams of protein to 10 grams of carbohydrates or less). If you're making your own meal replacement shake with protein powder, add it to milk or water. Remember that 8 ounces of milk contain about 7 grams of protein and 9 grams of carbohydrates. Therefore you'll need to account for the protein and carbohydrates in the milk.

LUNCH (NOON) AND DINNER (7:00 P.M.)
28 grams protein
10 grams carbohydrate

OPTION 1

Protein
Chicken (4–6 ounces), beef (4–6 ounces), pork (4–6 ounces), fish (6 ounces), *or* your favorite protein choice from the "Macronutrient Units" list (page 82). You may add approximately 1 tablespoon of your favorite sauce (barbecue, teriyaki, etc.) and your favorite spices.

Carbohydrate
Favorite vegetables *and/or* green salad: Choose 1 unit (9 carbohydrate grams) of your favorite vegetable listed on the "Macronutrient Units" list (page 84). You may combine several different vegetable as long as the total grams of carbohydrate add up to 1 unit (9 grams). Example: 1 cup of cauliflower and ½ cup of broccoli.

See "Food Preparation Tips" (page 67) for butter and salad dressing recommendations.

OPTION 2

Protein
Tuna (6 ounces), chicken (4–6 ounces), *or* egg salad (4–6 ounces) (with reduced-fat mayonnaise) **or lean deli meat (4–6 ounces).** You may also add cheese, lettuce, tomato, onion, pickles, or your favorite garnishes as long as you account for their protein and carbohydrate content.

Carbohydrate
Choose one of the following: 1 small tossed lettuce salad, 1 tomato, 1 medium-size avocado, ⅓ bagel, ½ English muffin, 1 low-carbohydrate tortilla, *or* 1 slice (low-carbohydrate bread). You may add mayonnaise and mustard to taste.

OPTION 3 (FAST-FOOD OPTIONS)

Garden fresh salad: 1 salad with your favorite protein choice (with your favorite dressing, no croutons)
Chicken or steak burrito: 1 burrito; order extra chicken or steak (no tortilla or ½ tortilla without rice and beans). Guacamole, salsa, and sour cream are fine in conservative amounts.

Chicken or steak soft taco: 1 soft taco; order extra chicken or steak (tear off ½ tortilla)

Deli-style or sub sandwich: 1 sandwich with your choice of meat or cheese (without top bun or protein style—wrapped in lettuce)

Grilled chicken sandwich: 1 grilled chicken sandwich (without top bun or protein style—wrapped in lettuce)

Rotisserie or grilled chicken: 1 skinless thigh, leg, or breast with 1 side coleslaw

Hamburger: ⅓ pound double hamburger or double cheeseburger (without top bun or protein style—wrapped in lettuce)

Pizza: 3 slices (don't eat the crust, eat only the toppings: cheese, meat)

You will maintain a low-fat diet naturally by making your protein choices from the "Best Choices" categories on the "Macronutrient Units" list (page 82).

SNACK (3:30 AND OPTIONALLY 11:00 P.M.)
7 grams protein
5 grams carbohydrate

OPTION 1

1 celery stalk filled with 1 tablespoon of natural peanut or other nut butter *or* 2 ounces cream cheese (reduced fat)

OPTION 2

Choose one of the following: 1 cheese stick (string cheese), **1 ounce cheese** (reduced fat), *or* **1 ounce lean deli meat with your favorite fruit**—choose ½ unit (4.5 carbohydrate grams) of your favorite fruit from the "Macronutrient Units" list (page 85).

OPTION 3

¼ cup nuts (any type)

OPTION 4

1 (6- to 8-ounce) hot or iced caffelatte (1% or 2% milk) **coffee drink** (sugar-free). Ask the coffee establishment to add a shot of flavored sugar-free syrup if available. You may also ask to blend your iced caffelatte in the blender with sugar-free syrup added for a sugar-free ice blended coffee drink. Some coffee establishments have pre-prepared sugar-free ice blended coffee drinks.

OPTION 5

1 (4- to 6-ounce) glass of milk (skim, 1%, or 2%)

OPTION 6

½ cup light yogurt (any flavor) *or* **½ cup plain yogurt** (you may add your favorite sugar-free syrup flavor). You may also choose a low-carb yogurt/dairy snack option (approximately 7 grams of protein to 5 grams of carbohydrates).

OPTION 7

½ 40-30-30 *or* **protein bar** (approximately 7 grams of protein to 5 grams of carbohydrates)

OPTION 8

Choose one of the following: 1 (4- to 6-ounce) glass of wine (dry red or dry white) *or* **1 light beer with one of the following: 1 cheese stick** (string cheese), **1 ounce cheese** (reduced fat), **1 ounce lean deli meat,** *or* **1 ounce turkey jerky** (low sodium).

OPTION 9

1 deviled or hard-cooked egg

OPTION 10

¼ cup ice cream (any brand or flavor) with 1 ounce cheese (reduced fat) *or* **¼ cup low-carb ice cream without cheese** (approximately 7 grams of protein to 5 grams of carbohydrates)

TOTAL HEALTH SUCCESS STORY

I Finally "Feel Good in My Skin"

TAMMY B.
Loving wife and mother

Tammy B. before

AGE: 32
HEIGHT: 5 FEET, 10 INCHES
TOTAL HEALTH START DATE: APRIL 2003
START WEIGHT: 253 POUNDS
AFTER WEIGHT: 188 POUNDS
TOTAL WEIGHT LOSS: 65 POUNDS
START BODY FAT PERCENTAGE: 40.4%
AFTER BODY FAT PERCENTAGE: 28.7%
START FAT POUNDS: 102.5
AFTER FAT POUNDS: 54
TOTAL POUNDS OF FAT LOSS: 48.5
START DRESS OR PANTS SIZE: 22
AFTER DRESS OR PANTS SIZE: 12/14

Tammy B. after

I happened upon Dr. Markham's Total Health plan about two years ago, when one of my good friends shared her secret of her 36-pound weight loss. At the time, I was nearing the end of my third pregnancy and obviously carrying a lot of added weight. I told myself that after I had the baby and finished nursing I was going to give Total Health a serious try. I had no idea how much it would change my life.

I'm 5 feet, 10 inches and have never been very skinny, always leaning more toward the athletic side. I had been a size 6 and never weighed more than 135–145 lbs. I was very active in sports in high school and fell into the bad habit of being able to eat anything I wanted without really giving it much thought, because I burned it all off through exercise.

I remember being told that someday I was going to have to watch it because my eating habits would eventually catch up with me. I always shook my head and plunged back into my hamburgers and fries. Fast-forward to thirteen years of marriage and three babies later, I found myself the heaviest weight I had ever been in my life at 246 pounds and a size 22. If that wasn't incentive enough to take to heart Dr. Markham's Total Health plan, I don't know what is.

I can remember the exact date I went to my first Total Health lecture. It was April 14, 2003. I sat surrounded by about fifteen or so other people watching Dr. Markham pull up all his visuals detailing his program as well as some of the before and after pictures. Several people at the dinner stood up to talk about how much their health and their overall lives had been changed by the Total Health plan, and I remember being mesmerized, realizing that I had finally found the cure for what ailed me!

From that point on, I wasn't just someone sitting at that lecture, I became a woman on a mission! I scheduled an appointment and private consultation with Dr. Markham for the very next day and from that point on began living and enjoying my life in a totally different way.

My husband, Charlie, knew I had attended the meeting, and as an added incentive to me (and I'm sure for some underlying motives of his own), he told me that he was going to start following the Total Health plan with me. He has always been so supportive of me and so completely nonjudgmental about my weight in general, and I think even he saw in me a change after that lecture.

I was serious about this! It was as if a lightbulb had turned on in my head, finally showing me how I'd been doing it all wrong all along. My husband was no skinny minny himself, at about 6 feet and 220 pounds. He wore a size 38 pants when he started Total Health.

My first week on the plan, I lost 7 pounds, and it just continued from there—5 pounds next, then 4 pounds, then 6 pounds . . . I remember the receptionist at my first appointment telling me that my weight was just going to "melt off." I remember actually rolling my eyes in disbelief. Each week I weighed in and lost more and more weight, and it was her turn to roll her eyes!

I must say that the support and sense of camaraderie of Dr. Markham's staff was one of the reasons I was so successful in the beginning. There is nothing like having someone pat you on the back each week after you've accomplished a 5-pound weight loss, so imagine how I felt when I had not only my husband but Dr. Markham's entire staff as well as Dr. Markham himself applauding me for my "job well done."

I will forever be grateful for that. There is a lot to be said for accountability, and if you are like me, accountability is *key* to success in most things in life, including weight loss. I found that my weekly weigh-ins at Dr. Markham's office were *monumental* in my success.

Once I realized that Dr. Markham's plan was a plan I could live with, I couldn't keep my mouth shut about it. After a couple of months, it became obvious I was doing something, and I was getting many questions about how I was losing all this weight and could I please share my "secret." And as my friend had done for me, I began converting as many people as I could to the Total Health plan.

Without even knowing it, I became sort of a walking billboard for the Total Health plan, living proof that it really worked. Not even the Internet was safe from me. I began recruiting women from my mom's groups online who then joined his online program at www.totalhealthdoc.com. Because of the changes that I made in my own life following Dr. Markham's Total Health plan, I now saw that Dr. Markham had changed many other people's lives as well—through me!

I am pretty sure that if you followed a trail starting from me on down through all the people I've turned on to the Total Health plan, you would find literally thousands of pounds lost. And I am just one person. I can't even begin to imagine how many total pounds have been lost through some type of direct or indirect contact with Dr. Markham's Total Health plan. Truly, it has changed lives.

As of right now, I have lost nearly 70 pounds in less than a year, have gone from a size 22 to a size 12–14. I am still going toward my goal of a size 10. My goal for weight loss was to lose 88 pounds total, and I have no doubt in my mind that I will achieve that. My husband has lost 55 pounds and now wears a size 30 pants! It's unbelievable.

Together, we have shed 125 pounds simply by following Dr. Markham's plan. It has literally changed our lives. I am exercising more. I am spending more time playing with my children at the beach instead of worrying about how I look at the beach, and I finally "feel good in my skin."

Dr. Markham's plan of eating works because it fits into our lives. It is easy to follow and never feels like a "diet." It just makes sense to me, and from the moment I started the plan, I have never looked back. I can't imagine ever going back to the way we ate before.

"Free" Snacks

Sugar-free Jell-O and homemade sugar-free Popsicles (made in a Popsicle mold with Crystal Light lemonade or sugar-free soda) are about the only acceptable free snacks. You may add some reduced-fat whipped cream to the Jell-O.

You may also eat some **low-carb, sugar-free chocolate bars** *or* **candies** with zero net carbs to satisfy your occasional sweet tooth, but not in un-limited amounts. They still contain calories, sugar alcohols, and fat.

Refer to Appendix B, "Recommended Products," for the best-tasting high-quality low-carb product brands available.

POWERFUL TIPS FOR REDUCING HOLIDAY FOOD CRAVINGS

Around the holidays I'm always asked the question "What can I have for holiday meals and still maintain a protein-rich, favorable-carbohydrate balance?" My response to my patients is not to worry about it, go ahead and enjoy your day. The key is to get back to a healthy balance of proteins and carbohydrates the very next day.

Keeping your blood sugar under control by limiting excessive carbohy-drate consumption will help reduce your food cravings, and you're less likely to continue eating your way through the holidays from Thanksgiv-ing through New Year's. Here are some powerful tips for keeping those car-bohydrate cravings under control during the holidays:

• Be sure to eat an adequate amount of the main protein entrée at your holiday meal. This is usually in the form of turkey, ham, duck, or some other meat. If you are unsure about how much protein to eat, you can use what I call the "ballpark" technique: keep your protein choice to a por-tion a little larger than the size of the palm of your hand—roughly 4–6 ounces.

• Go ahead and eat a small amount of each side dish. This would in-clude sweet potatoes, mashed potatoes and gravy, stuffing, cranberry sauce, etc. Even though we consider these forms of carbohydrates unfavorable, I want you to enjoy your day. Just eat a smaller amount of each than usual.

• Enjoy a small portion of dessert, such as pumpkin pie, immediately after the main meal. If you wait to have dessert later in the day, do not eat it by itself. You must have the dessert along with a protein such as cheese to counterbalance the blood sugar response to the dessert.

• Make sure to send all of the desserts and unfavorable-carbohydrate leftovers home with your guests. This will keep you from being tempted through the course of the day and the remainder of the holidays.

Part IV

Exercise:
How to Get Started and Why

Not getting enough exercise? You're not alone. The number of Americans whose idea of physical activity is reaching for the remote control has reached crisis proportions.

In 1996, a U.S. surgeon general's report estimated that 60 percent of adult Americans were not physically active on a regular basis. And 25 percent of adults—that's one in four Americans—were not active at all! In 1999, a follow-up survey conducted for a nonprofit weight loss support group reported that nearly half (48 percent) of Americans claimed to exercise regularly.

That figure—while encouraging—still leaves more than half of American adults on the couch. Is it any wonder that the number of people who are disabled or killed by obesity-related diseases grows every year?

If you're serious about living in Total Health, you must make regular physical activity part of your life. In this chapter, we'll take a look at how your body *and mind* benefit from a combination of aerobic, resistance, and passive exercise. You'll also learn insider tips on choosing a health club and working with a personal trainer.

WHY EXERCISE IS IMPORTANT

The benefits of regular physical activity are astounding. For starters, exercise increases your metabolism, which helps you burn fat. Exercise boosts your stamina, strength, and flexibility. It strengthens your bones and improves your posture. And it lowers your risk of developing heart disease, high blood pressure, stroke, and diabetes.

Physical activity also increases your self-esteem and confidence. You'll look better, and you'll feel better about the way you look. Exercise reduces stress, improves your mood, and helps you sleep better. New research also suggests that exercise may even stimulate brain cell growth and slow the aging process.

Your body needs to move. If you don't use it, losing it is just a matter of time. As you get older, even simple tasks such as climbing stairs will leave your lungs winded and your heart racing. Your joints will stiffen, and your bones will weaken. Injuries will occur more often—with more serious consequences. Your range of motion will also suffer. You'll have to watch the way you bend over to pick up the paper. Turning your neck to back your car out of the driveway will be a struggle.

If you doubt me, I suggest you spend a day in a retirement community. Talk to people who've learned about the importance of regular exercise the hard way. They'll tell you that no matter how busy you are, it's a lot easier—and a lot less painful—to work with a personal trainer now rather than a chiropractor or physical therapist later.

How Regular Exercise Burns Fat Faster

After thousands of Total Health consultations, I noticed that some of my patients consistently made faster progress toward their goals. What were these "fast track" patients doing differently? The "secret" was remarkably simple: *Patients who lost weight faster—and kept it off—made exercise a regular part of their weekly routine!*

While it's true that many people who follow the Total Health plan lose weight just by eating protein-rich, favorable-carbohydrate meals, following a regular exercise program turbocharges your body's ability to burn fat. Here's how . . .

First, exercise boosts your metabolism, the complex biochemical process by which food is converted into energy. The lower your metabolic rate, the harder it is for you to burn calories. The faster your metabolic rate, the easier it is to lose weight. More about how to speed up your metabolism in a moment.

Second—and more important—your body has a powerful hormonal response to exercise.

When you follow your Total Health eating program *and* commit to a regular exercise routine, your body becomes a fat-burning machine. Thanks to your body's hormonal response to a protein-rich, favorable-carbohydrate way of eating, your high glucagon levels are already mobilizing stored fat to be burned as energy. Burning body fat gives you more than twice the amount of energy as burning sugars does. The result is more energy for your workout.

The complete opposite is true when you "carbo-load" before a workout. Carbohydrates stimulate the release of insulin and inhibit the release of glucagon. Your workout is fueled by sugar, not by stored body fat.

There is another benefit of having high glucagon levels prior to exercise. Glucagon helps widen blood vessels, allowing your muscles access to more oxygen and nutrients. The result is a better workout and a faster recovery.

There are two basic types of active exercise: aerobic and resistance. If you want to lose unwanted body fat and gain lean, fat-burning muscle mass, you need to do both.

Aerobic Exercise

Aerobic exercise works your heart and lungs, improving your body's ability to use oxygen as an energy source, stimulating the release of glucagon—the fat-burning hormone—and inhibiting the release of insulin—the fat storage hormone. The goal is to increase your stamina by training your body to work more efficiently and use less energy to do the same amount of work. The sooner your heart rate and breathing return to resting levels after a workout, the better your conditioning.

Aerobic activities are continuous and rhythmic, such as walking, hiking, jogging, bicycling, and swimming. To benefit from aerobic exercise, you need to exercise at 60 to 80 percent of your maximum heart rate for 20 to 30 minutes at least three times a week. To figure your maximum heart rate, subtract your age from 220.

Example: If you're 60 years old, you would subtract 60 from 220 for a "maximum heart rate" of 160. So you would want to keep your heart rate in the 60 to 80 percent range of 96 to 128 beats per minute.

Caution: *Always consult with your physician before embarking on any form of aerobic exercise.*

There are two ways to measure your heartbeats per minute. One way is to count your pulse beats for 15 seconds, then multiply that number by four. The other is to invest in a heart rate monitor. Models vary in sophistication, from about $75 to more than $200.

Note: Refer to Appendix C, "Exercise Resources," heart rate monitor recommendations.

Resistance Exercise

Pumping iron may seem like a mindless activity, but your body gains tremendous benefits from it. Resistance exercise or weight training builds your muscular strength, endurance, definition, and tone. In the process, it also develops stronger bones and improves your posture. Most important, lifting weights accelerates your metabolism.

How many times have you heard people say that the reason they can't lose weight is because they have a slow metabolism? Or listen to others explain that the reason they never gain weight is a naturally fast metabolism? The implication is that your metabolic rate—fast or slow—is a matter of genetic fate and out of your control.

That's just not true. Metabolism is a function of muscle mass. If you have the metabolism of a napping snail, it's because you have a low ratio of muscle tissue to fat tissue.

This is why resistance exercise using resistance bands or weights must be part of your workout routine. The more lean muscle mass you have, the higher your metabolism. The faster your metabolism, the easier it is for your body to burn—and avoid storing—fat. Even when you're resting!

Resistance exercise tears down muscle fiber, which stimulates the pituitary gland to release *human growth hormone*. Human growth hormone is broadly recognized by the scientific and medical community as one of the body's most powerful hormones. Longevity experts believe it may be the key to reversing the effects of aging. It's also known as a ferocious fat burner.

Human growth hormone mobilizes stored body fat to strained muscles, where it is burned as energy to repair torn muscle fiber. It's during this healing process that muscles gain bulk, tone, and definition.

Resistance exercise fuels your body's natural fat-burning cycle. Human growth hormone burns more fat and builds more muscle, which makes it even easier for your body to burn more fat. And every time you lift weights, this amazing process repeats itself!

And you thought pumping iron was just for guys named Moose!

Passive Exercise

Passive exercise is essential for proper muscle and joint health. It increases your flexibility—your ability to bend, stretch, and twist easily. It improves your balance and coordination, and it reduces your risk of injury. Regular passive exercise may even slow the progression of osteoarthritis and other degenerative joint conditions.

There are two kinds of passive exercise: do-it-yourself stretching exercises and the muscle and joint mobilization performed by a qualified health care professional, such as a doctor of chiropractic. As you age, muscle stretching and joint mobilization will help preserve and improve your mobility and range of motion.

Stretching before and after workouts will help you avoid pulled muscles, cramps, and a variety of other injuries. It will also speed your recovery. Moist heat and a skilled massage or physical therapist can do wonders to loosen knots and tight muscles.

Your joints also need special attention. As you age, calcium salts seep into the joints, causing accelerated wear much the same way sand wears down gears in a machine. This contributes to a condition called osteoarthritis, which over time often leads to restricted movement.

Maintaining mobility is one of the keys to longevity and aging gracefully. Many entertainment and sports celebrities have extended their careers and preserved their range of motion well into their seventies and eighties thanks to periodic massage and joint mobilization.

Think of all the preventive maintenance it takes to keep your car running. Oil changes every 3,000 miles. New tires every 50,000 miles. A new timing belt around 75,000 miles. Not to mention all the spark plugs, filters, and fluids that are replaced according to the service schedule.

You understand that if you don't take care of your car, it will be only a matter of time before it breaks down for good. Now, if money is no obstacle and you can't be bothered with maintenance, when your car stops running, you can just go out and buy another. There are always plenty of cars available.

The human body is the most complicated machine in the world—and you get only one of them. If you want to get the most from yours, take care of it. Give yourself the fuel you need. Exercise. And put yourself on a regular joint maintenance schedule. In the long run, you'll find it's a lot easier—and less expensive—to stay healthy than to keep your car running.

CHOOSING A HEALTH CLUB

Deciding to start an exercise program is easy. Making exercise part of a life-long commitment to fitness is another matter. The key is to schedule a regular time for exercise and then stick to your schedule until exercise becomes a habit. For most people, the *minimum* amount of time it takes to develop a natural exercise habit is six weeks. That's one hour of focused exercise three times a week for six weeks.

Too many people start exercising filled with unrealistic goals and expectations. And when they don't see dramatic weight loss, rock-hard abs, or "buns of steel" after a couple of weeks, they get discouraged. They procrastinate. They get distracted by other priorities. Before long, they're back on the couch.

If you're serious about living in Total Health and you want to make exercise part of your lifestyle, consider joining a health club. There are a number of advantages:

- **Focus and motivation:** Once you're at the health club, you've overcome the number one obstacle to sticking with a regular exercise program: showing up. Now you have no more excuses. You're not distracted by the phone, the laundry, the kids, or myriad household chores. You're there to work out. And so is most everyone else. It's really hard to procrastinate when everyone around you is in motion.

- **Equipment choices:** Good health clubs invest in a variety of top-quality aerobic and resistance training equipment. You'll find several ways to get an aerobic workout or work a muscle group. That means it's easy to try out new exercises and equipment when it's time to freshen up your workout routine. And the more choices you have, the easier it is to stick with your exercise program.

- **Relaxation:** If you want to give your mind a rest, put your body to work. Many of my patients report that time spent at the gym is deeply relaxing. Their focus is on simple physical tasks, such as lifting weights and breathing properly. Workouts are an oasis in a day of obligations.

Is joining a health club expensive? Only if you don't use your membership. To make sure you choose a club that's right for you, consider the following before signing a membership agreement:

- **Location:** Join a club that's convenient to home or work. It's too easy to avoid working out if your club is too far out of your way.

- **Hours:** Will you be able to work out at a time that's convenient for you? Can you take advantage of less crowded off-peak times?
- **Cleanliness:** Check out the bathrooms and showers. Remember, it's supposed to be a *health* club. That means the facilities are cleaned regularly. Better clubs clean their changing, shower, and restroom facilities throughout the day.
- **Staff:** Do the people behind the reception counter greet you with a smile? Do they make eye contact? Or are they too busy comparing tans and muscle mass to notice you? You want to feel comfortable asking them for help. After all, you'll be paying for it.
- **Atmosphere:** Does everyone in the club look like a professional bodybuilder? Are there both men and women working out? What kind of music is playing and how loud? Does the staff make an effort to "walk the floor" to answer questions or offer training tips? Each club has a distinct "personality." In this way, joining a health club is a little like having a roommate: you get along great, you put up with each other, or you move out.
- **Stretching area:** Is there a separate area in which to stretch before your workout?
- **Weight room:** Are there enough free weights and weight machines to go around? What about cardiovascular equipment such as stair-climbers, treadmills, stationary bikes, rowing and skiing and elliptical motion machines? Is the equipment clean and in good repair? You want to be able to spend your time working out, not waiting in line.
- **Aerobics:** Does the club offer aerobics classes? If so, ask for a class schedule. If you plan on being the Sultan of Step or the Queen of Kickboxing, make sure the only class isn't offered at 5 A.M. (unless you're an early-morning person). Also, ask about the aerobics instructor's certification. Look for credentials from the American Council on Exercise (ACE), the Aerobic Fitness Association of America, or the Exercise Safety Council.

Some health clubs also provide extras:

- **Sports leagues:** Many clubs organize basketball, volleyball, and racquetball leagues.
- **Swimming pools:** Check chlorination levels and cleaning schedules. Are swimming and water aerobics courses offered? How many lap lanes are available throughout the day and during lessons?
- **Child care services:** More and more clubs are offering on-site child

care for parents who need someone to watch their kids while they work out. Many clubs contract with experienced day care companies to maintain and staff the club's child care facilities. Even so, make sure you check out the child care facility and staff with the same scrutiny you'd apply to a full-time day care center. At a minimum, the staff must be certified for infant and child CPR training. Ask about fire, emergency, and security procedures. Are staff required to have background checks? How often are toys and equipment cleaned? Ask about the sickness policy. Get the answers you need to have peace of mind that your children will be safe and happy while you're taking some time for your own health and happiness.

• **Orientation tours:** Some clubs offer free orientation tours to show new members how to use the equipment. Make sure the advice comes from a certified personal trainer—not the receptionist.

• **Personal training programs:** Many clubs offer one-on-one sessions with a personal trainer as an additional service. Working with a personal trainer is a great way to stay motivated and focused during your workout. Most clubs offer a complimentary training session and fitness evaluation to entice you to sign up for a series of personal training sessions. Others also throw in nutritional supplements and high-energy bars. But those incentives won't matter if you don't choose the right personal trainer for you. And that leads us to . . .

HOW TO CHOOSE A PERSONAL TRAINER

Health clubs are overflowing with free advice from well-meaning members. The problem is that much of it is misguided or just plain wrong. It can also be dangerous. Push yourself too hard on a treadmill, lift too much weight, or use bad form, and you're bound to hurt yourself.

Learning how to exercise safely and efficiently is a good reason for working with a personal trainer. Hiring a personal trainer also makes sense if:

• You want to stay motivated and focused.
• You want a fitness routine customized to help you reach your health goals.

These days, a lot of people are calling themselves personal trainers. The hard part is choosing a personal trainer who's right for you. Here are some tips and criteria to keep in mind:

- **Credentials:** There was a time when all you needed to call yourself a personal trainer was a good body and a business card. Today, professional personal trainers are certified by nationally recognized fitness organizations. Look for credentials from the American College of Sports Medicine (ACSM), the American Council on Exercise, the Institute for Aerobics Research, or the National Strength and Conditioning Association.

- **Educational background:** Want to work with a trainer who is committed to his or her profession? One indication is a bachelor's degree in health or exercise science. You also want someone who keeps up to date on fitness training and health information. Ask prospective trainers if they subscribe to any professional journals or attend continuing education classes or seminars.

- **CPR/first aid training:** If something goes wrong during your workout, can your trainer do more for you than dial 911?

- **Personality:** You are hiring a personal trainer to give you the motivation and information you need to benefit from a fitness routine. Being positive and enthusiastic is part of a personal trainer's job description. What matters is how that enthusiasm is expressed through a trainer's personality. There's a huge difference between nonstop bubbly and nonstop intensity. You'll be paying this person to spend a lot of time with you, so make sure you have a good rapport.

- **Communication skills.** An effective personal trainer needs superb communication skills. You want a trainer who listens to your concerns and who takes the time to explain things in a way that you can understand. A trainer with a Ph.D. in exercise science is useless if he or she can't communicate knowledge in a way that makes sense to you. There is no such thing as a stupid question. If a trainer makes you feel otherwise, find another trainer.

- **Gender:** Training is an up close and personal activity. You may prefer to work with a trainer of either the same or the opposite sex.

- **Fees:** Expect to pay between $50 and $100 an hour for a personal trainer. Ask about reduced rates for multiple sessions. What is the trainer's cancellation policy? How and when are you billed?

- **Availability:** Can the trainer accommodate your schedule? If you're not a morning person, don't expect yourself to get up at 5:30 A.M. to sweat with Sven.

THE PRINCIPLES BEHIND CIRCUIT TRAINING

The concept of group exercise is not new. Arthur Jones, the inventor of Nautilus fitness equipment, first introduced circuit training or group exercise concepts back in the 1970s, and these are now becoming popular once again.

Fitness centers have been using the group exercise format for many years under many names (dance aerobics, step classes, cycling programs, etc.). The principle is very simple: It's more fun to work out with your friends or others in a group scenario. Fun and camaraderie are key elements to the success of any group situation.

One of the fastest-growing fitness franchises in the world offers a 30-minute circuit training course. All of the equipment is hydraulic, and there are no weights to add or remove. The object is to keep the heart rate going, so half of the time you do aerobics on boards or steps and half the time you use strength-training equipment.

This means you can get a complete fat-burning, muscle-toning, cardiovascular workout in just 30 minutes. The workout is performed in an interval circuit format (work/recover/work/recover) with timed intervals (usually 30 to 45 seconds) at each station. Usually a total of 9 to 13 resistance stations is used. These pieces use hydraulic cylinders designed to provide the amount of resistance you require for the type of exercise you desire.

Hydraulic resistance is the only type of resistance that is "accommodating" in nature; that is, the resistance matches the effort of the user, even as the user fatigues during exercise. The principle is similar to that of aquatics; the faster one tries to move fluid, the greater the resistance. You're much less susceptible to injury on this type of equipment. When (and if) you give out, it stops immediately. That's why almost anyone can perform this type of exercise, including athletes, executives, busy moms, dads, kids, the overweight, and seniors.

I was so impressed with the effectiveness and safety of this type of exercise that I now provide this type of equipment for my patients at the Total Health Weight Loss, Wellness and Chiropractic Center in Thousand Oaks, California.

Suggestions on Starting Your Exercise Program

Option 1

If you haven't been involved in a structured exercise program in the past and finances aren't a problem, I suggest joining a local circuit training gym or health club with a certified trainer to show you how to exercise.

Option 2

If finances are a concern or time is a factor, I recommend my 30-Minute "Fat-Burning" Circuit Training Workout (see below).

The following section includes photographs of and instructions on performing proper warm-up and stretching exercises, along with my 30-Minute "Fat-Burning" Circuit Training Workout. I developed this program, based on circuit training exercise, during my high school All-American wrestling days in the 1970s. This unique exercise system can be performed at home or on the road using a bungee resistance exercise band.

THE 30-MINUTE "FAT-BURNING" CIRCUIT TRAINING WORKOUT

Congratulations on embarking on your new exercise program! I recommend exercising three days per week: Mondays, Wednesdays, and Fridays. This gives your body a day of rest between exercise sessions. On Tuesdays and Thursdays you can, for example, go for an evening walk after dinner for a relaxed form of enjoyable, nonaggressive exercise. Weekends should be reserved for nonstructured, fun recreational activities of your choice, depending on the season and weather, such as golf, waterskiing, hiking, bicycling, swimming, surfing, snow skiing, etc. This will give you a well-rounded and reasonable way to incorporate a healthy blend of physical activity into your busy lifestyle.

The 30-Minute "Fat-Burning" Circuit Training Workout consists of 9 different exercises that work all the major muscle groups. These include the back, stomach, shoulders, arms, legs, and chest. You perform 3 sets of 12 repetitions of each exercise in addition to walking or running in place with the resistance of the bungee device for 30 to 45 seconds in between each set of exercises.

The workout takes approximately 30 minutes if you walk or run for 30 seconds in between each set of resistance exercises, 45 minutes if you walk or run for 45 seconds.

Step One: Warming Up

A proper warm-up enhances your body's vasodilation (opening up of the blood vessels) so that more blood supply is delivered to your muscles. Since warm muscles are more elastic, they're less susceptible to injury. Warm muscles also have a fluidlike stretch that allows for a greater range of motion, whereas cold muscles don't absorb shock or impact as well. Therefore, it's very important to warm up your muscles properly even before stretching them prior to starting any exercise program.

The most common way to warm up your muscles prior to stretching is by walking or marching in place while swinging your arms for 3 to 5 minutes. The best way to know that your body is properly warmed up for stretching is that you begin to perspire lightly. Once you have begun to perspire, you are ready to begin your stretching routine.

Step Two: Stretching

When you begin a stretching exercise, go to the point where you feel a mild tension and relax as you hold the stretch. **Do not bounce!**

Perform the following stretches in the following order:

Psoas Stretch
Lying on your back, bend your knees with your feet on the floor and flatten your lower back against the floor. Next, bring one knee to your chest by clasping your hands on top of or behind the knee and pulling with your arms until you feel a stretching in your buttocks. Gradually straighten the opposite leg. Hold the stretch for 10 seconds and then repeat with the other leg.

Low Back Stretch

Lying on your back, bend your knees with your feet on the floor and flatten your lower back against the floor. Next, bring both knees to your chest by clasping your hands on top of or behind both knees and pulling with both arms until you feel a stretching in your buttocks. Hold the stretch for 10 seconds.

Twisting Low Back Stretch

Lying on your back, bend at the knees with both feet on the floor. Let your knees go to the left and your head and torso to the right. Hold the stretch for 10 seconds, feeling the stretch in your low back muscles. Repeat again for 10 seconds on the opposite side.

Back Extension

Lie on your stomach with your arms extended above your head, legs straight, toes pointed. Slowly push your upper body off the floor by straightening your arms. Breath deeply and relax your pelvis so that it drops down into the stretch. Hold the stretch for 10 seconds.

Hamstring Stretch

Sitting on the floor, straighten your right leg as you keep your left leg bent. The sole of your left foot should be facing the inside of your upper right leg; you are in a straight-leg, bent-knee position. Now, to stretch the back of the upper right leg (hamstrings) bend forward chest first from the hips until the slightest, easiest feeling of stretch is created. Hold the stretch for 10 seconds. Repeat for 10 seconds on the opposite side.

Groin Stretch
Sit on the floor. Put the soles of your feet together with your hands around your feet and toes. Now gently pull your upper body forward until you feel an easy stretch in your groin area. You may also wedge your elbows in between your knees and apply a gradual outward pressure to achieve an additional stretch in the groin area. Hold the stretch for 10 seconds.

Foot and Ankle Stretch
While sitting, rotate your ankle clockwise and counterclockwise through a complete range of motion with slight resistance provided by your hand. Moving your ankle in a rotary motion helps to gently stretch tight ligaments. Repeat 10 to 20 times in each direction. Next, use your fingers to gently pull your toes toward you to stretch the top of the foot. Hold the stretch for 10 seconds. Repeat again for 10 seconds with the opposite foot and ankle.

Arm and Shoulder Stretch

Sitting on the floor, bend at the knees and lean back on your hands with your arms stretched out behind you. Next, lift your buttocks off the floor and rock slowly forward and backward, feeling the stretch in your shoulders and the back of your arms. Rock back and forth 10 to 20 times.

Calf Stretch

Face a fence, wall, or other vertical surface that you can lean on for support. Stand a little distance from this support and rest your hands on the support above your head. Now bend one knee and bring it toward the support. The back leg should be straight, with the foot flat and pointed straight ahead. Without changing the position of your feet, slowly move your hips forward as you keep your back leg straight and your foot flat. Create an easy feeling of stretch in your calf muscle (gastrocnemius). Hold the stretch for 10 seconds. Repeat again for 10 seconds with the opposite calf.

Step Three: Attaching the Bungee Cord

The bungee device consists of a six-foot-long bungee cord with a grip handle on each end. In the middle of the bungee cord is a nylon attachment loop that is used to attach the exercise device to a standard doorknob or a sturdy railing.

Refer to Appendix C, "Exercise Resources," for resistive exercise equipment recommendations.

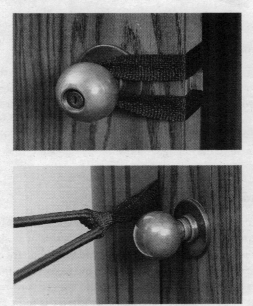

Doorknob Attachment

When using a doorknob as your attachment site, simply slip the attachment loop strap over the doorknob and close the door securely, with the bungee device pulling into the door frame.

Railing Attachment

When using a railing as your attachment site, make sure the railing is sturdy. This will more than likely be the upright (vertical) post at the end of the railing, which anchors into the floor. Wrap the bungee cord around the sturdiest portion of the railing, feeding both handles of the bungee device through the open loop of the attachment loop strap, and pull tight for a secure attachment to the railing, as shown.

Step 4: Aerobic Walking or Running in Place

Once the bungee device is securely fastened to either the doorknob or railing, you are ready to start the bungee exercise routine by walking or running in place. First hold the handle of one end of the bungee cord in your right hand and the other handle in the left hand facing away from the door or railing attachment site. You may have the bungee cord resting either outside your arms or inside your arms, whichever is most comfortable. Next, walk away from the attachment site, creating some tension on the bungee cord.

Note: The further you walk from the bungee attachment site, the more tension you create on the bungee. If you haven't been exercising regularly, you should start out with less tension on the bungee and work up to more tension later, as you begin to get into better shape. This will help to reduce potential muscle pulls, soreness, and so forth. Also, be sure not to walk or run on your toes too much, as this may lead to pulls or excessive soreness in the calf muscles of your legs.

Once you've created the desired tension on the bungee cord, you may

start walking or running in place. After you've walked or run in place for 30 to 45 seconds, you'll be ready for your first set of resistance exercises.

Step Five: Resistance Band Exercises

There are nine different sets of resistance exercises, designed to tone the muscles of the back, stomach, shoulders, arms, legs, and chest. Twelve repetitions equals one set, and you should perform three sets each of the nine different exercises. After each set, walk or run in place. The nine exercises and the order in which they should be performed are as follows.

Caution: Not all exercise programs are suitable for everyone. Always consult your physician before beginning this or any other exercise program. If at any time you feel you're exercising beyond your current fitness abilities or you feel discomfort, you should discontinue the exercise immediately.

Back Extension

With the bungee attached to the doorknob or railing, sit on the floor facing the bungee attachment site with your knees slightly bent and your feet shoulder width apart. Hold the bungee handles close together, with your left and right hands overlapping each other. Then pull the handles to your chest. Remember, the further away you are from the bungee attachment site, the more tension there will be on the bungee cord, so don't sit too far away from the attachment site in the beginning. Once you've pulled the bungee handles to your chest, simply extend backward against the resistance of the bungee cord, as shown. When you perform this exercise properly, you'll feel resistance in your lower back muscles.

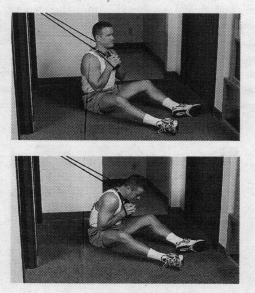

Stomach Crunch

With the bungee attached to the doorknob or railing, sit on the floor facing away from the bungee attachment site, with your knees slightly bent and your feet shoulder width apart. Bring one bungee handle over your right shoulder and the other handle over your left shoulder. While continuing to hold the handles, link the fingers of your right and left hands together in front of your chest, creating a tight grip on the bungee handles. Slide away from the bungee attachment site to create your desired tension and bend or crunch forward against the resistance of the bungee cord. When you perform this exercise properly, you'll feel the resistance in your stomach muscles.

Shoulder Shrugs

Detach the bungee from the doorknob or railing and hold one handle in each hand. Allow the bungee to hang down to the floor in front of you. Stand on the bungee with your feet approximately shoulder width apart. With your arms at your sides, shrug your shoulders up and backward against the resistance of the bungee cord. The closer your feet are to the handles on the bungee cord, the more resistance you will create. When you perform this exercise properly, you'll feel the resistance in your trapezius muscles (the ones that connect your neck to your shoulders).

Note: You will have to reattach the bungee to the door or railing attachment site between sets (12 repetitions) of shoulder shrugs to perform the aerobic portion (walking or running in place) of the bungee workout. This also pertains to all other bungee resistance exercises where you're required to detach the bungee.

Anterior Deltoids

Detach the bungee from the doorknob or railing and hold one handle in each hand. Allow the bungee to hang down to the floor in front of you. Stand on the bungee with your feet approximately shoulder width apart. Now hold the bungee handles by squeezing them together in front of you with your right and left hands. Keeping your hands close to your body, pull the handles up to your chin against the resistance of the bungee cord. When you perform this exercise properly, you'll feel the resistance in your anterior (front) shoulder muscles.

Biceps

Detach the bungee from the doorknob or railing and hold one handle in each hand. Allow the bungee to hang down to the floor in front of you. Stand on the bungee with your feet approximately shoulder width apart. Now perform an arm curl against the resistance of the bungee with your right arm and then your left arm. When you perform this exercise properly, you'll feel the resistance in your biceps muscles.

Triceps

With the bungee attached to the doorknob or railing, face the bungee attachment site with one handle in each hand. Bend your knees and lean slightly forward while backing up to create tension on the bungee cord. Now, with your arms bent at a 45° angle next to your body, extend first your right arm backward and down and then your left arm. Your elbow joints act as hinges while you straighten each arm against the resistance. When you perform this exercise properly, you'll feel the resistance in your triceps muscles.

Seated Rows

With the bungee attached to the doorknob or railing, sit on the floor facing the bungee attachment site with your knees slightly bent and your feet shoulder width apart. Holding one bungee handle in each hand, slide backward, creating tension on the bungee cord. Now simply pull the bungee handles to your stomach against the resistance of the bungee cord while maintaining an upright seated posture. This exercise is designed to strengthen the latissimus dorsi muscles in your back.

TOTAL HEALTH SUCCESS STORY

I Tried the Atkins Diet and Failed

RUSTY N.
Instrument technologist

AGE: 40
HEIGHT: 5 FEET, 4 INCHES
TOTAL HEALTH START DATE: APRIL 2004
START WEIGHT: 167 POUNDS
AFTER WEIGHT: 156 POUNDS
TOTAL WEIGHT LOSS: 11 POUNDS
START BODY FAT PERCENTAGE: 20%
AFTER BODY FAT PERCENTAGE: 15.8%
START FAT POUNDS: 33.5
AFTER FAT POUNDS: 24.5

Rusty N. before   *Rusty N. after*

TOTAL POUNDS OF FAT LOSS: 9
START WAIST MEASUREMENT: 32 INCHES
AFTER WAIST MEASUREMENT: 30 INCHES

I had decided to do something about my weight, and I knew absolutely nothing about exercise or nutrition. I had been very active in my youth with bicycles and motocross, so I could eat and drink whatever I wanted and it didn't seem to affect me much. I joined the Navy in 1987 and weighed 154 pounds. I was already a bit chubby at that point, as I am only 5 feet, 4 inches tall. I quickly gained 10 pounds and for eight years struggled to maintain my weight at 164 pounds.

This was the cutoff for mandatory physical fitness training on a weekly basis. I would starve and dehydrate myself for weeks to make my weight. I was often just a bit over, and they would let me slide.

When I got out of the Navy in 1995, I had no reason to watch my weight. I quickly soared to nearly 189 pounds. I decided to try spinning classes. I figured I could spin seven days a week and eat whatever I wanted, just as I had in my youth. I lost a few pounds and got a little stronger, but there was not much of a noticeable difference.

My exercise program came to a halt in March 2001, when I broke my leg below the knee and dislocated my ankle, destroying most of the cartilage. I was in a cast up to my hip. The damage in the ankle was not discovered until

June 2001. Surgery was scheduled for September. I was stuck in a beanbag chair from March 18 until December 11.

I had to do something; I was blowing up like a balloon. I decided to cut out refined sugar and make protein shakes with fruit and nuts. I lost some weight, but I was still pushing 180 pounds. I tried limiting my calorie intake, but I never got very good results for any length of time.

In April 2003, I tried the Atkins diet and failed. I was able to hit 160 pounds but always crept back up to 170 pounds. I could not live on the Atkins high-fat protein choices and little- to no-carb "induction phase" forever. I wasn't getting any further in my weight loss, and I didn't like the idea of not being able to eat fruit in the "induction phase" of the Atkins plan.

In April 2004, I was referred to Dr. Markham by a coworker who had read his book. I went to see him on April 13. His approach seemed logical and more balanced—not too restrictive, but the same principles as I had learned with other protein-rich diets.

His program also outlined the specific amount of protein I needed at each meal and allowed fruit in the initial weight loss phase. I weighed in at 167 pounds, 20 percent body fat. The day I left his office I went to check out the gym after reading about how his clients who exercised had good results.

So I started spinning and weight training. Realizing that I had no idea what I was doing with my training routine, I hired a personal trainer. I made a lot of mistakes in my first weeks of training. I was overtraining, not allowing my body to recover, and I had no idea about how to train efficiently and properly.

Most of all, I was not listening to what my body needed. Despite these mistakes I still lost weight and felt better. In four weeks I was down to 155 pounds and from 20 percent body fat to 18 percent. In six weeks I was up to 159 pounds but down to 16.9 percent body fat. In eight weeks I was at 156 pounds and 15.8 percent body fat.

I am a very active person, and for several years I have struggled to get enough sleep. I am now waking up before my alarm clock and staying up later than ever. I have more energy and feel stronger than I ever have. Not only do I feel physically balanced, but I also feel an emotional balance due to my new eating habits and exercise lifestyle.

Knee Bends

Detach the bungee from the doorknob or railing, and hold one handle in each hand. Allow the bungee to hang down to the floor in front of you. Stand on the bungee with your feet approximately shoulder width apart. With your arms at your sides, bend your knees at a 45° angle and pull the bungee cords up waist high. Now stand up straight. The closer you stand to the handles, the more resistance you will create. This exercise is designed to strengthen the quadriceps muscles in your legs.

Chest

With the bungee attached to the doorknob or railing, face away from the attachment site with one handle in each hand. The bungee cord should rest on the outside of your arms. Walk away from the bungee attachment site, creating the desired amount of tension on the cord. Bend slightly at the knees and push your arms forward against the resistance of the bungee cord. This exercise is designed to strengthen your chest muscles.

Part V

Mental Health:
Helpful Hints for Happiness

One of the principles of the Total Health program is that your mental health is just as important as your physical health. Here are some tips on how to preserve your emotional and social well-being and the importance of intellectual and spiritual growth.

EMOTIONAL AND SOCIAL WELL-BEING

Seek out and nurture healthy relationships. Choose your friends carefully. Look for people who value honesty and integrity. Look for people who build you up, not bring you down. Life is hard enough without inviting unhealthy, energy-draining personal and business relationships into your life.

Suppose you're a recovering alcoholic. In the past, you'd get drunk with the same group of friends on a regular basis. Now that you're trying to stay sober, you probably don't want to surround yourself with people who prefer to hang out in bars. And as much as you may like your old drinking buddies, the smarter choice is to cultivate friendships with people who understand your addiction and who support your decision not to drink.

When it comes to business relationships, it doesn't matter whether you're a doctor, a mechanic, or a roofing contractor. Eventually, we all face situations that raise moral and ethical dilemmas. Your life is directed by the choices you make. It isn't always easy to make the right ones. The important thing to realize is that you do have choices!

INTELLECTUAL DEVELOPMENT

Commit to a lifetime of learning—professionally and personally. Want financial success? Provide increasingly better service to your customers or clients. Keep up with your profession's or trade's new trends, techniques, and equipment. Attend continuing education seminars. Read professional journals and books. It doesn't matter whether you treat patients or repair cars. Strive to become the best at what you do. Your investment will pay off in greater self-esteem, confidence, job satisfaction, and income.

Balance professional development with personal growth. Stimulate your brain with hobbies and activities that spark creativity. Write, draw, paint, play music, play chess, dance, sing. Too busy? Give your creative time the same respect you give your professional time. Pull out your day planner and set aside time for fun!

Bonus. Spend quality time with the most important people in your life by involving your spouse, significant other, or children in your creative endeavors. You never know when you might spark a shared interest. That's what happened to me when my uncle came to visit. He was an artist, and he always brought sketch pads and pencils for me and my siblings. Then he'd teach us how to draw. When I was four years old, he taught me how to play chess. I don't draw like Rembrandt or play chess like Kasparov, but that's not the point. Thanks to my uncle's gift of time, I discovered two creative outlets that I enjoy to this day.

SPIRITUAL GROWTH

Contemplate your life's purpose. What are you here for? When you aren't clear about your life's purpose, you're likely to pass through life without direction. This lack of focus often leads to poor personal and business decisions, poor career choices, relationship problems, depression, eating disorders, substance abuse, and a host of other life-draining distractions.

When you're clear about your life's purpose, you can focus your energy on achieving meaningful goals and dreams. Figuring out your purpose in life takes time and determination. Consider the following suggestions to help you get started . . .

Make time for self-renewal. Set aside time on a daily basis to reflect on your purpose, dreams, and goals in life. If you believe in God or a higher power, you can pray for direction on how you can best use your talents to fulfill your purpose in life. It doesn't matter where you are—at home, commuting to work, on the golf course, in the shower—you can always take a few minutes to reflect on who you are, what you have accomplished in life, and how you fit into the big picture.

Tip. Spend your self-renewal time focusing on love and goodness. Don't you spend enough time thinking about how much you have to do and how little time you have to do it in? Isn't it demoralizing to watch the anger, injustice, and violence on the nightly news? You cannot control the actions of others. But you can control your own thoughts and actions. Choose to dwell on what's right and good for a few minutes each day. It's good for the soul.

Love and serve others. This is one of the best ways to begin to discover your life's purpose. Regardless of your economic background, age, race, or religion, you can love and serve others by showing concern and giving your time to people who are less fortunate.

Most of us won't live up to the good deeds of Mother Teresa, but we can experience the same joy and goodness just by serving the people closest to us. Nowhere is this principle's power more evident than in its ability to shape the lives of children.

How do we describe a parent's job? A parent *raises* or *brings up* a child. Think about that for a moment. The job description calls for parents *to raise* children, *to bring them up*. Not tear them down. One of the easiest ways to bring children up is to praise them for the things they do right!

You don't have to be a parent to make a tremendous impact on a child's life. Do you know any single mothers or fathers who are struggling to raise children? Simple gestures, such as including their kid in your own family function, can make all the difference.

I know because it happened to me. My dad left my mom when I was seven. I had two older brothers and a younger sister. My mom had spent fifteen years as a housewife. She had no marketable skills—and now she had to support us. She went to work for minimum wage. There was no money for child care.

Fortunately, our neighbors across the street were concerned about our sudden change in fortune. They went out of their way to keep a close eye on me and my siblings while Mom was at work. And they included us in many of their family activities. I remember going waterskiing and snowmobiling with them. My neighbors even took me along on their summer vacations.

It meant—and still means—the world to me that they opened their hearts to me. Over the years, I've come to realize that in many ways, they saved my life. Without a father and with a mom who worked all the time, I needed the security of knowing that someone cared. Who knows what kind of choices I would have made in life if I hadn't had that security and love to fall back on?

Maybe my late grandmother's simple advice sums it up best. She said, "Every time I get depressed or start to feel sorry for myself, I just do something nice for someone else. It makes me feel a lot better." Thank you, Grandma Markham!

Serve your community. Community service is another great way to love and serve others. If you have kids in school, get involved and help support programs that improve the quality of education. Help with after-school programs that offer kids positive activities that keep them out of trouble.

Community-based organizations such as the YMCA, Boy Scouts, Girl Scouts, and teen centers help kids develop leadership and teamwork skills. They also promote healthy ideas about the value of service to others. Business and civic organizations such as Rotary International, Kiwanis, Optimists, Lions Clubs, and American Legion also give back to the community by raising money for a wide range of community service organizations.

ONE MORE THING

All of us come from different backgrounds and different life experiences. These experiences can fill our lives with light and joy—or they can trap us in unhealthy and sometimes dangerous behaviors. If you suffer from behaviors or addictions that are keeping you from realizing your life's potential, you owe it to yourself and your loved ones to seek professional help. If money is an issue, there are many city-, county-, state-, and federally funded programs that can help. There are also many twelve-step support programs, such as Alcoholics Anonymous (AA), Adult Children of Alcoholics (ACOA), and Overeaters Anonymous (OA), that meet on a regular basis.

Part VI

Total Health Recipes

PROTEIN-RICH APPETIZERS AND SNACKS

Zucchini-Cheese Squares

1 garlic clove, minced
6 eggs, beaten
1 small onion, chopped
3 cups shredded Cheddar cheese
2½ cups shredded zucchini
½ cup olive oil or safflower oil
½ teaspoon salt
½ teaspoon basil
½ teaspoon oregano
¼ teaspoon pepper
½ cup grated Parmesan cheese
⅓ cup bread crumbs
¼ cup sesame seeds, toasted

Preheat the oven to 325°. Sauté the onion and garlic in oil until almost limp. Add the zucchini and cook until tender-crisp. Mix the eggs with the bread crumbs, spices, Cheddar cheese, and zucchini. Spread into a greased 9-by-13-inch baking dish. Sprinkle with the Parmesan cheese and sesame seeds. Bake for 30 minutes or until set when touched lightly in the center. Cool at least 15 minutes. Cut into 1-inch squares and serve warm, at room temperature, or cold.   Makes 10 dozen squares (120 squares)

NUTRITIONAL FACTS PER SERVING
Protein: 2 grams
Carbohydrates: 1 gram

Turkey Roll-Up

1 ounce turkey
1 green olive, stuffed with pimiento

This is a great way to use leftover holiday turkey. Slice the turkey into thin strips. Wrap each strip around an olive and spear with a toothpick. Ready for dipping into your favorite sauce.   Makes 1

NUTRITIONAL FACTS PER SERVING
Protein: 7 grams
Carbohydrates: 1 gram

Smoked Salmon Rolls

4 ounces cream cheese
1 tablespoon lemon juice
1 tablespoon grated onion
Freshly ground black pepper
Chopped parsley
2 slices smoked salmon

Have the cheese at room temperature and mix in the lemon juice, grated onion, and a little pepper. Blend until very soft. Spread on slices of salmon, roll up like a Swiss roll, and cut into 2-inch pieces. Chill several hours. Dip both ends of the rolls in chopped parsley before serving.   Serves 6

NUTRITIONAL FACTS PER SERVING
Protein: 6 grams
Carbohydrates: 1 gram

Salmon-Stuffed Avocados

1 8-ounce package cream cheese, softened
2 7½-ounce cans salmon, drained
3 avocados, black or green
1 tablespoon lemon juice
2 teaspoons Worcestershire sauce
1½ teaspoons salt
⅛ teaspoon pepper

In a large bowl, with a wooden spoon, beat the cream cheese with the salmon, Worcestershire sauce, salt, and pepper until fluffy. Halve the avocados lengthwise and remove the pits. Brush the cut sides with lemon juice to prevent discoloration. Fill the hollow of each half with the cream cheese mixture. Refrigerate until well chilled, about 1 hour.   Serves 6

NUTRITIONAL FACTS PER SERVING
Protein: 11 grams
Carbohydrates: 5 grams

Jiffy Tomato Stack-Ups

3 large tomatoes
4 ounces Swiss cheese, shredded
10 ounces package chopped broccoli, cooked and drained
¼ cup chopped onion

Cut the tomatoes into slices about ¾ inch thick. Sprinkle each slice lightly with salt. Set aside 2 tablespoons of the shredded cheese; combine the remaining cheese, broccoli, and onion. Place the tomato slices on a baking sheet and spoon the broccoli mixture onto the tomatoes. Sprinkle with the reserved cheese. Broil 7 to 8 inches from heat for 10 to 12 minutes, or until the cheese bubbles and the tomato slices are hot.   Serves 6

NUTRITIONAL FACTS PER SERVING
Protein: 6.5 grams
Carbohydrates: 6.6 grams

Herbed Olives

2 cups unpitted ripe or green olives
2 small hot, dried red chilies
2 garlic cloves
2 tablespoons finely chopped celery leaves
2 tablespoons capers, drained
12 leaves rosemary
1 bay leaf
1 cup olive oil

Place the olives in a jar, interspersed with all the ingredients except the oil. Pour in enough oil to cover. Cover the jar and shake well. Refrigerate 3 or 4 days before using; shake the jar several times during this period. Remove the garlic if the olives are stored for any length of time.   Makes 3 cups

NUTRITIONAL FACTS PER SERVING
Protein: 0 grams
Carbohydrates: 1 gram

Ham Roll-Ups

1 ounce thinly sliced ham
1 ounce square Cheddar or Swiss cheese

Wrap the ham around the cheese squares. Serve with your favorite mustard for dipping.   Makes 1

NUTRITIONAL FACTS PER SERVING
Protein: 14 grams
Carbohydrates: 0 grams

Crab-Stuffed Mushrooms

8-ounce package cream cheese, softened to room temperature
1 tablespoon chopped green onion
½ cup crabmeat, drained and flaked
½ teaspoon Worcestershire sauce
½ pound fresh mushrooms, cleaned, with stems removed
¼ cup grated Parmesan cheese

In a mixing bowl, combine all ingredients except for mushrooms and Parmesan cheese. Stuff mushrooms with crab mixture, mounding the tops slightly. Sprinkle with Parmesan cheese. Bake at 350° until filling is golden (about 20 minutes).   8 servings

NUTRITIONAL FACTS PER SERVING
Protein: 2 grams
Carbohydrates: 1 gram

Beef Roll-Up

1 ounce roast beef, thinly sliced
1 stuffed green olive

Wrap the beef around the olive and spear with a toothpick. Serve with Dijon mustard horseradish sauce.   Makes 1

NUTRITIONAL FACTS PER SERVING
Protein: 7 grams
Carbohydrates: 1 gram

Avocado and Crabmeat Cocktail

1 avocado
1 6-ounce can crabmeat
3 scallions, finely chopped
1 tablespoon light mayonnaise
1 teaspoon olive oil
½ teaspoon salt
½ teaspoon pepper
½ teaspoon nutmeg
½ teaspoon paprika

Chop avocado and add the crabmeat, scallions, mayonnaise, oil, salt, pepper, and nutmeg. Mix and serve in a cocktail glass over ice, sprinkled with paprika.

Serves 2

NUTRITIONAL FACTS PER SERVING
Protein: 14 grams
Carbohydrates: 5 grams

Spicy Grilled Shrimp

2 pounds medium-sized shrimp
1 teaspoon chili powder
1 tablespoon vinegar
¼ teaspoon pepper
1 garlic clove, minced or mashed
1 teaspoon salt
1 teaspoon basil
1 tablespoon finely chopped fresh mint or 1 teaspoon dried mint
¾ cup safflower oil

Wash, shell, and devein the shrimp (or use about 1½ pounds frozen deveined large shrimp; they need not be thawed). In a bowl or glass jar, blend the chili powder with the vinegar, pepper, garlic, salt, basil, and mint. Stir in the oil and shake or mix until well blended. Pour over the shrimp, cover the dish, and marinate in the refrigerator for at least 4 hours or overnight. Thread the shrimp on skewers and grill over charcoal for 6 to 10 minutes (depending on size), turning once and basting liberally with the marinade. (Or arrange unskewered shrimp on a broiler rack and broil in the oven, turning once and basting well.)

Makes about 50 appetizers, or 6 servings as a main dish

NUTRITIONAL FACTS PER SERVING
Protein: 37 grams
Carbohydrates: 1 gram

SALADS AND SOUPS

❖ ❖ ❖ Salads ❖ ❖ ❖

Chicken Caesar Salad

1 garlic clove
¾ cup olive oil
4 chicken breasts
2 large heads romaine lettuce
½ teaspoon salt
Freshly ground black pepper
2 eggs, boiled 1 minute and cooled
Juice of 1 large lemon
6 to 8 anchovy fillets, chopped
½ cup grated Parmesan cheese

Crush the garlic in a small bowl, pour the oil over and let stand several hours. Cut each chicken breast into 4 lengthwise strips, stir fry, and set aside. Tear the romaine into a large salad bowl and sprinkle with the salt and a generous amount of pepper. Pour ½ cup garlic oil over the salad and mix until every leaf is glossy. Break the boiled eggs into the salad; squeeze the lemon juice over and mix thoroughly. Add the anchovies, chicken, and cheese. Mix again and serve.   Serves 4

NUTRITIONAL FACTS PER SERVING
Protein: 28 grams
Carbohydrates: 8 grams

Cold Asparagus Salad

4 cups water
1 pound asparagus, cut diagonally
1 garlic clove, chopped fine
2 tablespoons light soy sauce
2 tablespoons sesame seed oil
¼ teaspoon Splenda

Bring the water to a boil in a wok. Drop the asparagus in and boil 1 minute. Drain and rinse with cold water. Mix the remaining ingredients in a bowl and pour over the asparagus. May be kept in a covered jar in the refrigerator about a week.   Serves 4

NUTRITIONAL FACTS PER SERVING
Protein: 0 grams
Carbohydrates: 5 grams

Cauliflower Salad

2 cups cauliflower, broken into florets
½ cup chopped, pitted ripe olives
⅓ cup finely chopped green pepper
¼ cup chopped pimiento
3 tablespoons chopped onion

DRESSING
4½ tablespoons safflower oil
1½ tablespoons lemon juice
1½ tablespoons wine vinegar
1 teaspoon salt
¼ teaspoon Splenda
Dash pepper

In a medium bowl, combine the cauliflower, olives, green pepper, pimiento, and onion. To make the dressing, in a small bowl, combine the oil, lemon juice, vinegar, salt, Splenda, and pepper; beat with a rotary beater until well blended. Pour the dressing over the cauliflower mixture and refrigerate until well chilled, at least 1 hour. Keep covered. To serve, spoon the salad into a bowl or arrange on lettuce on individual salad plates.

Serves 4

NUTRITIONAL FACTS PER SERVING
Protein: 0 grams
Carbohydrates: 5 grams

California Coleslaw

4 cups finely shredded cabbage
½ cup thinly sliced celery
½ cup chopped cucumber
2 tablespoons chopped green pepper
2 tablespoons sliced green onions
1 tablespoon chopped parsley
1 tablespoon lemon juice
¼ cup mayonnaise
¼ cup light sour cream
½ teaspoon salt
½ teaspoon Splenda
Dash pepper
Dash paprika
1 avocado

Combine the cabbage with the celery, cucumber, green pepper, onions, and parsley. To make the dressing, combine the lemon juice, mayonnaise, sour cream, salt, Splenda, pepper, and paprika; mix until smooth. If you make the dressing ahead, cover and refrigerate it until serving time. Just before serving, peel the avocado and dice it. Add the diced avocado and dressing to the salad and mix lightly.

Serves 6

NUTRITIONAL FACTS PER SERVING
Protein: 1 gram
Carbohydrates: 6 grams

Avocado and Red Onion Salad

2 heads Boston lettuce, washed and chilled
1 ripe avocado
1 large red onion
4 ounces olive-oil-and-vinegar dressing

Break the lettuce into a salad bowl in bite-sized pieces. Peel the avocado and cut large pieces into the salad bowl. Peel and slice the onion thinly and add to the salad bowl. Toss with oil-and-vinegar dressing just before serving.   Serves 6

NUTRITIONAL FACTS PER SERVING
Protein: 1.3 grams
Carbohydrates: 6.6 grams

Seafood Salad

1 cup flaked cooked halibut
1 cup flaked cooked crabmeat
1 cup chopped celery
½ cup mayonnaise
¼ cup chopped sweet pickle
2 tablespoons lemon juice

Combine all the ingredients and chill thoroughly. Serve in lettuce cups.
                                          Serves 2

NUTRITIONAL FACTS PER SERVING
Protein: 12 grams
Carbohydrates: 5 grams

Curried Chicken Salad

1 pound diced chicken, both light and dark meat
1 Granny Smith apple, diced
1 teaspoon chicken base
1 heaping teaspoon curry powder
½ teaspoon garlic powder
½ teaspoon coarsely ground black pepper
Mayonnaise to taste

Mix all the ingredients. Stir in mayonnaise to taste.   Serves 4

NUTRITIONAL FACTS PER SERVING
Protein: 21 grams
Carbohydrates: 5 grams

Marinated Zucchini Salad

1½ cups beef broth
8 medium zucchini
16 cherry tomatoes
Boston or red leaf lettuce
1 4-ounce can ripe olives, sliced

ZESTY MARINADE
½ cup olive oil
⅓ cup wine vinegar
3 teaspoons Dijon mustard
¾ teaspoon salt
¼ teaspoon pepper
3 tablespoons chopped green pepper
3 tablespoons chopped green onion
3 tablespoons chopped parsley
1 teaspoon dry tarragon

In a wide saucepan, bring the beef broth to a boil. Add whole zucchini. Return to a boil. Cover and cook 8 minutes, or until the zucchini are barely tender when pierced with a fork. Do not overcook; they will soften as they marinate. Remove the zucchini from the heat and immediately plunge into ice water to stop cooking. Drain, cool, and cut lengthwise into eighths. Place in a 9-by-13-inch glass baking dish. Add tomatoes and pour the marinade over. Cover with plastic wrap and refrigerate overnight. To serve the salad, line a large platter or individual salad plates with lettuce leaves and place the zucchini on top. Cut the tomatoes in half and arrange around the zucchini. Garnish with sliced olives and drizzle additional marinade over.

To make the marinade, in a blender or food processor fitted with the metal blade, combine the oil, vinegar, mustard, salt, and pepper until blended. Place in a small bowl. Stir in the green pepper, onion, parsley, and tarragon.   Serves 4

NUTRITIONAL FACTS PER SERVING
Protein: 1 gram
Carbohydrates: 5 grams

Oriental Coleslaw

½ large head cabbage, coarsely shredded
4 green onions, thinly sliced
¼ cup slivered almonds
¼ cup sesame seeds
1 teaspoon salt
1 teaspoon pepper
¾ cup olive or safflower oil
6 tablespoons rice vinegar

Lightly roast the almonds and sesame seeds in a saucepan on the stove. Combine all the ingredients and toss with a dressing made of the oil and rice vinegar.   Serves 4

NUTRITIONAL FACTS PER SERVING
Protein: 2 grams
Carbohydrates: 7 grams

❖ ❖ ❖ **Dressings** ❖ ❖ ❖

Creamy Garlic Dressing

> 2 medium garlic cloves, chopped
> 1 egg
> ¾ cup olive oil or safflower oil
> ¼ cup wine vinegar
> ½ teaspoon salt
> ¼ teaspoon pepper

In a blender, combine all the ingredients and blend until creamy and smooth. Chill several hours or overnight. Serve on greens of your choice.

Makes about 1¼ cups

NUTRITIONAL FACTS PER SERVING
Protein: 2 grams
Carbohydrates: 0 grams

Greek Dressing

> ½ cup olive oil
> ½ cup crumbled feta cheese or cottage cheese
> 3 tablespoons wine vinegar
> ½ teaspoon oregano

Combine all the ingredients and mix well. Chill several hours or overnight. Serve on greens of your choice.   Makes 1 cup

NUTRITIONAL FACTS PER SERVING
Protein: 2 grams
Carbohydrate: 0 grams

Italian Vinaigrette

¾ cup olive or safflower oil
¼ cup wine vinegar
1 large garlic clove, crushed
1 teaspoon salt
½ teaspoon dry basil
½ teaspoon dry oregano

Combine all ingredients and mix well. Chill several hours or overnight. Serve on greens of your choice.   Makes about 1 cup

NUTRITIONAL FACTS PER SERVING
Protein: 0 grams
Carbohydrate: 0 grams

❖ ❖ ❖ **Soups** ❖ ❖ ❖

Cold Guacamole Soup

  ½ cup milk
  2 avocados
  1 green pepper, chopped
  1 small onion, chopped
  2 tablespoons lemon juice
  1 teaspoon sea salt
  3 cups plain yogurt
  Mint leaves or parsley for garnish

Blend all the vegetables with milk in a blender. When smooth, add the yogurt. Chill. Serve garnished with mint or parsley.   Serves 4

NUTRITIONAL FACTS PER SERVING
Protein: 7 grams
Carbohydrates: 12 grams

Gazpacho

----

    4 large ripe tomatoes, peeled and chopped
    1 large cucumber, peeled and diced
    1 medium-size onion, finely minced
    1 green pepper, seeded and finely minced
    1 cup tomato juice, cold water, or regular-strength chicken broth
    1 small garlic clove, mashed or minced
    3 tablespoons olive oil
    1 tablespoon wine vinegar
    Salt and pepper to taste

Mix the tomatoes, cucumber, onion, green pepper, tomato juice, vinegar, oil, and garlic; add salt and pepper to taste. Chill the soup until icy and serve well chilled.   Serves 6

NUTRITIONAL FACTS PER SERVING
Protein: 1 gram
Carbohydrates: 8 grams

Zucchini Soup

----

    3 pounds zucchini, cubed
    3¼ cups water
    4 strips bacon, cut fine (don't precook)
    1 bouillon cube
    1 onion, chopped
    1 small garlic clove
    Salt and pepper to taste

Boil all the ingredients in a sauce pan until tender, approximately 1 hour. Blend the cooked ingredients in a blender and serve.   Serves 4

NUTRITIONAL FACTS PER SERVING
Protein: 5.5 grams
Carbohydrates: 6.5 grams

PROTEIN-RICH ENTRÉES

❖ ❖ ❖ Beef ❖ ❖ ❖

Prime Rib

2 bulbs garlic, cloves peeled
1 teaspoon salt
6½ pounds prime rib roast, fat trimmed off in one strip and reserved
12 bay leaves
Pepper
2 cups red wine

Preheat the oven to 450°. Puree the garlic in a blender or food processor fitted with a steel blade. Add salt to the garlic and process to a paste. Pat the garlic paste over the top and sides of roast in an even layer. Place the bay leaves evenly over the garlic. Place the trimmed strip of fat over the garlic and bay leaves. Tie in place with kitchen string. Sprinkle the roast all over with salt and pepper to taste. Place in a roasting pan and pour red wine into the bottom of the pan. Roast 20 minutes per pound for medium done. Let stand 5 minutes before carving.   Serves 8

NUTRITIONAL FACTS PER SERVING
Protein: 28 grams
Carbohydrates: 1 gram

Oven-Baked Spareribs

3 tablespoons hoisin sauce
2 tablespoons dark soy sauce
2 tablespoons light soy sauce
2 tablespoons honey
1 tablespoon sherry
1 tablespoon tomato ketchup
1 tablespoon Splenda
1 garlic clove, chopped fine
2 pounds spareribs, cut lengthwise into 3 pieces

Preheat the oven to 350°. Combine all ingredients but the spareribs in a shallow dish or pan. Add the spareribs and marinate overnight. Line a shallow pan with aluminum foil. Roast the ribs 45 minutes. Turn the heat down to 325° and roast for another 15 minutes. When shrinkage occurs, the ribs are finished.   Serves 4 to 6

NUTRITIONAL FACTS PER SERVING
Protein: 24 grams
Carbohydrates: 2 grams

Mexican Steak

4 steaks, about 6 ounces each
2 garlic cloves, pressed
1 large onion, sliced
1 pound mushrooms, sliced
9 ounces beef broth
9 ounces red wine
4 small cans green chili salsa

Layer a baking dish with the steaks, garlic, onion, and mushrooms. Mix the broth, wine, and salsa together. Pour over the top and bake at 350°F for 1 hour, or until done.   Serves 4

NUTRITIONAL FACTS PER SERVING
Protein: 42 grams
Carbohydrates: 4 grams

Company Flank Steak

2 pounds flank steak

STEAK MARINADE
3 tablespoons honey
2 tablespoons vinegar
2–3 green onions, top and all
1 teaspoon garlic powder
1 teaspoon fresh ginger, grated
¾ cup olive oil
¼ cup soy sauce

Blend all marinade ingredients in the blender. Marinate the steak at least 24 hours. Barbecue the steak with plenty of marinade. Delicious!

Serves 8

NUTRITIONAL FACTS PER SERVING
Protein: 24 grams
Carbohydrates: 2 grams

Beef with Bean Sprouts

½ pound flank steak, shredded
1 teaspoon salt
1½ teaspoons cornstarch
4 tablespoons olive oil
2 cups bean sprouts
1 tablespoon sherry
2 tablespoons light soy sauce
1 teaspoon Splenda dissolved in 2 teaspoons water (if needed)

Combine the beef, ½ teaspoon of the salt, cornstarch, and 1 tablespoon of the oil. Mix well with your hands. Heat 2 tablespoons of the oil to 400° in the wok. When hot, stir-fry the beef 2 minutes. Remove, set aside, and wipe out the wok. Heat 1 tablespoon oil to 400° in the wok and stir-fry the bean sprouts. Add ½ teaspoon salt and stir-fry 1 minute more. Add the beef, sherry, soy sauce, and Splenda. Stir constantly for 2 minutes. If it is too watery, thicken with cornstarch until it reaches the desired consistency.

Serves 4

NUTRITIONAL FACTS PER SERVING
Protein: 28 grams
Carbohydrates: 2 grams

Wok Beef and Broccoli

- 1 tablespoon cornstarch
- 1 tablespoon soy sauce
- 1 cup lean, tender beef, sliced
- 1 garlic clove, chopped
- 2 tablespoons olive oil
- 2 cups broccoli stalks, thinly sliced across the grain
- 2 ounces canned mushroom pieces
- ½ teaspoon salt
- ⅓ cup beef soup stock

Combine the cornstarch, soy sauce, and beef and mix together in a mixing bowl. Stir-fry the garlic in oil; add the beef mixture, stir-fry, and remove. Add the broccoli, mushrooms, salt, and stock to the wok and bring to a boil. Cover the wok, reduce heat, and cook for about 4 minutes. Add the beef to the wok and cook 1 to 2 minutes with cover removed. Serve at once.

Serves 2

NUTRITIONAL FACTS PER SERVING
Protein: 28 grams
Carbohydrates: 10 grams

Hungarian Goulash

3 large onions, thinly sliced
1 tablespoon olive oil
1 teaspoon caraway seeds
½ teaspoon marjoram
1 teaspoon salt
2–4 teaspoons paprika
1 teaspoon vinegar
2 pounds boneless beef chuck, cut in 1-inch cubes
1 cup dry red wine

Sauté the onions in oil until tender and golden; add the caraway seeds, marjoram, salt, and paprika moistened with the vinegar; mix well. Add the meat and brown nicely on all sides. Add the wine, cover tightly, and simmer very slowly for about 2 hours, or until the meat is tender. Add water during cooking, if necessary.　　　　　　　　　　　　　　Serves 8

NUTRITIONAL FACTS PER SERVING
Protein: 28 grams
Carbohydrates: 2 grams

Beef and Mushroom Stew

---

2 tablespoons olive oil
1½ pounds stew beef, cubed
1 can beef broth
1 cup water
¼ cup catsup
1 tablespoon prepared mustard
1 large garlic clove, pressed or minced
Dash Tabasco sauce
½ teaspoon salt
Generous dash pepper
2 large onions, quartered
1 small green pepper, chopped
1½ cups sliced mushrooms
2 tablespoons flour

Heat the olive oil over medium heat. Add the beef and brown on all sides. Pour off the fat. Add the broth, water, catsup, mustard, garlic, Tabasco sauce, salt, and pepper. Cover and simmer 1½ hours. Add the onions and cook 40 minutes more. Add the green pepper and mushrooms and cook 20 minutes more. Gradually blend ¼ cup water into the flour until smooth. Slowly stir into the stew. Cook, stirring, until thickened.   Serves 4

NUTRITIONAL FACTS PER SERVING
Protein: 35 grams
Carbohydrates: 4 grams

❖ ❖ ❖ **Pork** ❖ ❖ ❖

Stuffed Pork Tenderloin

4 ounces fresh mushrooms
1½ pounds pork tenderloin
Salt
Pepper
7-ounce jar or can roasted red peppers, drained
¼ cup chopped fresh parsley
2 tablespoons olive oil
3 garlic cloves, minced
1 cup chicken broth
2 tablespoons soy flour
2 tablespoons dry white wine or sherry

Finely chop 2 ounces of the mushrooms; slice the remaining 2 ounces and set aside. Cut the tenderloin almost in half lengthwise, leaving a ½-inch hinge. Open and lay flat. Pound to ¼-inch thickness and sprinkle with ½ teaspoon salt and ½ teaspoon pepper. Top with the roasted peppers in a single layer and sprinkle with the parsley and mushrooms. Roll up and secure with string. Salt and pepper the pork. Heat the olive oil in a skillet over medium-high heat. Add the pork and brown 2 minutes on each side; add the garlic during the last minute. Add the broth; sprinkle with salt and pepper. Reduce heat to medium; cover and simmer for 20 minutes. Remove the pork and keep warm. Increase heat to medium high and bring the pan juices to a boil. Add the sliced mushrooms and the wine or sherry; cook until slightly thickened. Serve over the pork.   Serves 6

NUTRITIONAL FACTS PER SERVING
Protein: 28 grams
Carbohydrates: 5 grams

Fresh Pork and Sauerkraut

3 pounds lean fresh pork
1 medium-size can or jar of sauerkraut
4 to 6 garlic cloves, minced
1 cup water

Trim any fat from the pork and cut into bite-size cubes. Drain the sauerkraut and rinse with water. Melt the fat trimmed from the fresh pork in a skillet and sauté the pork cubes until lightly browned. Add the minced garlic, sauerkraut, and water. Cover and bring to a boil. Simmer for 2 hours or until the meat is tender, stirring occasionally.   Serves 4

NUTRITIONAL FACTS PER SERVING
Protein: 42 grams
Carbohydrates: 5 grams

Peppers Stuffed with Pork

1 pound ground pork
½ teaspoon salt
3 tablespoons light soy sauce
1 tablespoon sherry
1 slice ginger, chopped fine
1 scallion, chopped fine
¼ cup water
1½ teaspoons cornstarch, dissolved in 1 tablespoon water
¼ cup oil
8 small green peppers
1 cup chicken stock
½ teaspoon Splenda

Combine the pork with the salt, 1 tablespoon of the soy sauce, the sherry, ginger, scallion, and water, and the cornstarch-water mixture. Mix well. Remove stems from the peppers. Cut holes at the top and remove the seeds. Wash the peppers thoroughly and dry them. Fill the peppers with the pork mixture. Heat the oil to 350° in a wok. Stir-fry the peppers

1 minute. Add 2 tablespoons of the soy sauce, the chicken stock, and the Splenda. Bring to a boil. Turn heat down and simmer 20 minutes.

Serves 4

NUTRITIONAL FACTS PER SERVING
Protein: 28 grams
Carbohydrates: 4 grams

❖ ❖ ❖ **Poultry** ❖ ❖ ❖

Asian Lemon Chicken

2 tablespoons dry sherry
1 tablespoon soy sauce
Four 3-ounce skinless, boneless chicken breasts
½ cup chicken broth
2 tablespoons fresh lemon juice
2 teaspoons cornstarch
2 teaspoons sesame oil
1 tablespoon peeled and chopped fresh ginger

In a medium bowl, combine the sherry and soy sauce; add the chicken, tossing to coat thoroughly. Let stand 10 minutes. In a small bowl, combine the broth, lemon juice, and cornstarch, stirring until cornstarch is dissolved; set aside. In a large nonstick saucepan, heat the oil. Add the ginger and cook, stirring constantly, for 2 minutes. Add the chicken and cook 2 minutes on each side, until golden brown. Stir the broth mixture and bring the liquid to a boil. Cook, stirring frequently, for 1 minute, until the liquid thickens slightly.   Serves 4

NUTRITIONAL FACTS PER SERVING
Protein: 21 grams
Carbohydrates: 1 gram

Barbecued Chicken

2 cups water
½ cup vinegar
6 garlic cloves, peeled
½ teaspoon freshly ground black pepper
One 2-pound chicken, skinned and cut into 4 equal parts

BARBECUE SAUCE
⅓ cup catsup
1 tablespoon light brown sugar
1 tablespoon grated onion
2 teaspoons cider vinegar
1 teaspoon Worcestershire sauce
1 teaspoon Dijon mustard

To prepare the marinade, combine 2 cups water with the vinegar, garlic, and pepper in a gallon-size plastic bag. Add the chicken; seal the bag, squeezing out any air; turn to coat the chicken. Refrigerate at least 2 hours or overnight, turning the bag occasionally. Place a grill rack 5 inches from the coals and prepare the grill according to the manufacturer's directions. To prepare the barbecue sauce, in a small saucepan, combine the catsup, brown sugar, onion, vinegar, Worcestershire sauce, and mustard. Bring to a boil; reduce heat to low and simmer 5 minutes. Set aside. Drain the marinade off and discard it. Grill the chicken 10 minutes. Brush both sides with barbecue sauce and grill 10 to 15 minutes longer, turning and brushing with the remaining sauce, until cooked through.   Serves 4

NUTRITIONAL FACTS PER SERVING
Protein: 28 grams
Carbohydrates: 4 grams

Chicken with Forty Cloves of Garlic

    40 garlic cloves
    2 tablespoons olive oil
    One 3-pound chicken, skinned and cut into 8 pieces
    ½ teaspoon salt
    ¼ teaspoon dried thyme leaves
    ¼ teaspoon dried rosemary leaves
    ½ cup chicken broth
    2 tablespoons minced flat-leaf parsley
    ½ teaspoon coarsely ground black pepper

Preheat oven to 350°. Spray a 9-by-13-inch baking pan with olive oil. In the prepared pan, combine the garlic and oil, tossing well to coat thoroughly. Bake 20 to 30 minutes, stirring every 10 minutes, until golden brown (be careful not to burn the vegetables). Sprinkle the chicken with salt, thyme, and rosemary; place in a baking pan with the garlic mixture. Pour the broth into the pan; bake, covered tightly, 50 to 60 minutes, until the chicken is cooked through and the juices run clear when a thigh is pierced with a fork. Transfer the chicken to a serving platter. With a slotted spoon, transfer the garlic to a food processor or blender; puree, slowly adding the pan juices, until very smooth. Stir in the parsley and pepper; pour over the chicken.   Serves 8

NUTRITIONAL FACTS PER SERVING
Protein: 42 grams
Carbohydrates: 2 grams

Dijon Mustard–Grilled Chicken Cutlets

    2 tablespoons olive oil
    3 tablespoons Dijon mustard
    2 teaspoons fresh lime juice
    1 teaspoon teriyaki sauce
    1 garlic clove, finely minced
    Pinch of ground red pepper
    Four 3-ounce skinless, boneless chicken breasts

Spray an indoor ridged grill pan with olive oil. In a medium bowl, with a wire whisk, combine the mustard, lime juice, teriyaki sauce, garlic, and pepper. Dip the chicken breasts into the mixture, one at a time, coating both sides; place on the prepared pan. Grill the chicken, brushing with remaining mustard mixture, 4 minutes on each side, until cooked through and the juices run clear when the chicken is pierced with a fork.

Serves 4

NUTRITIONAL FACTS PER SERVING
Protein: 21 grams
Carbohydrates: 2 grams

Macadamia Nut Chicken

    4 skinless, boneless chicken breasts
    2 eggs, beaten
    1 to 1½ cups crushed macadamia nuts
    2–3 tablespoons olive oil

Pound the chicken breasts until thin. Dip into the eggs and coat with macadamia nuts. Heat the oil in a nonstick skillet and sauté the chicken until done, approximately 8 to 10 minutes.   Serves 4

NUTRITIONAL FACTS PER SERVING
Protein: 21 grams
Carbohydrates: 4 grams

Chicken Sauté with Watercress

        4 teaspoons peanut oil
        10 ounces skinless, boneless chicken breasts, cut into 8 pieces
        2 cups onions, thinly sliced
        4 garlic cloves, minced
        8 cups watercress, finely chopped
        ¼ cup beef broth
        2 teaspoons Worcestershire sauce
        ¼ teaspoon salt
        ¼ teaspoon black pepper

In a large skillet, heat 2 teaspoons of the oil and add the chicken. Cook over medium heat 2 minutes on each side, until golden brown. Remove the chicken from the skillet and set aside. In the same skillet, heat the remaining 2 teaspoons oil. Add the onions and cook, stirring frequently, for 3 to 4 minutes, until lightly browned. Add the garlic and cook, stirring constantly, 2 minutes longer. Add the watercress to the onion mixture and cook, tossing constantly for 30 seconds, until wilted. Transfer the mixture to a serving platter and keep it warm. To the same skillet, add the broth, Worcestershire sauce, salt, pepper, and chicken. Cook, basting the chicken with pan juices, until the chicken is cooked through. Arrange the chicken on top of the watercress; top with the pan juices.   Serves 4

NUTRITIONAL FACTS PER SERVING
Protein: 18 grams
Carbohydrates: 2 grams

Mandarin-Stuffed Cornish Hens

1 large mandarin orange, peeled and sectioned
½ cup thinly sliced onion
⅓ cup balsamic vinegar
1 teaspoon dried oregano leaves
½ teaspoon salt
½ teaspoon black pepper
Two 1-pound Cornish game hens, skinned

Preheat the oven to 450°. Spray a 9-by-13-inch pan with olive oil. In a small bowl, combine the orange sections, onion, vinegar, oregano, salt, and pepper. Stuff the hens with equal amounts of the mixture, leaving most of the liquid in the bowl. Place the stuffed hens in a prepared baking pan and surround them with any remaining stuffing mixture. Baste the hens with some of the remaining stuffing liquid. Cover the pan with aluminum foil and bake, covered, for 30 to 35 minutes, basting several times with the remaining stuffing liquid, until the hens are cooked through and the juices run clear when a thigh is pierced with a fork. Remove the hens and any solid stuffing mixture to serving platter; set aside and keep warm. Drain the pan juices and any remaining basting liquid into a small saucepan and bring to a boil. Remove from heat and pour over the stuffed hens. To serve, cut the hens in half.   Serves 4

NUTRITIONAL FACTS PER SERVING
Protein: 42 grams
Carbohydrates: 5 grams

Spicy Chicken and Snow Peas

1 tablespoon Worcestershire sauce

1 tablespoon water

2 teaspoons sesame oil

2 teaspoons soy sauce

1 teaspoon Splenda

1 teaspoon cornstarch

1 teaspoon rice wine vinegar

¼ teaspoon crushed red pepper flakes

10 ounces skinless, boneless chicken breasts, cubed

2 teaspoons peanut oil

1 cup minced scallions

1 tablespoon chopped, pared fresh ginger

⅛ teaspoon Asian chili paste

1 cup snow peas (Chinese pea pods), stem ends and strings
    removed

1 tablespoon sesame seeds

1 teaspoon hoisin sauce

In a medium bowl, combine the Worcestershire sauce, water, sesame oil, soy sauce, Splenda, cornstarch, vinegar, and pepper flakes, stirring until the cornstarch is dissolved. Add the chicken, tossing well to coat thoroughly; let stand 10 minutes. In a wok or large skillet, heat the oil; add the scallions, ginger, and chili paste. Stir-fry 1 minute. Add the chicken mixture and stir-fry 4 to 5 minutes, until the chicken is cooked through. Add the snow peas, scallions, sesame seeds, and hoisin sauce; stir-fry 2 to 3 minutes longer, until the snow peas are tender.   Serves 4

NUTRITIONAL FACTS PER SERVING
Protein: 18 grams
Carbohydrates: 5 grams

Herbed Lemon Chicken

10 ounces skinless, boneless chicken breasts, cut into ¼-inch strips
1 egg white, beaten
3 tablespoons plain dry bread crumbs
¼ teaspoon dried thyme leaves
¼ teaspoon dried oregano leaves
¼ teaspoon salt
¼ teaspoon pepper
2 teaspoons unsalted butter
2 teaspoons peanut oil
½ cup chicken broth
2 tablespoons dry white wine
2 tablespoons fresh lemon juice
1 tablespoon capers, rinsed and drained
1 tablespoon minced fresh flat-leaf parsley
Lemon slices for garnish

In a medium bowl, combine the chicken and egg white, tossing well to coat the chicken thoroughly; set aside. In a gallon-size sealable plastic bag, combine the bread crumbs, thyme, oregano, salt, and pepper; seal the bag and shake to blend. Add 1 chicken slice, seal the bag, and shake to coat. Place the coated chicken slice on a large plate. Repeat, using the remaining chicken slices. In a large skillet, heat the butter and oil; when the foam subsides, add the coated chicken slices. Cook 1 minute on each side, until golden brown and cooked through. Transfer the chicken to a serving platter and keep warm. To the same skillet, add the broth, wine, lemon juice, and capers; cook over medium-high heat 2 to 3 minutes, until reduced to about ½ cup. Stir in the parsley and pour the mixture over the chicken. Serve garnished with lemon slices.

Serves 4

NUTRITIONAL FACTS PER SERVING
Protein: 18 grams
Carbohydrates: 1 gram

❖ ❖ ❖ **Fish and Seafood** ❖ ❖ ❖

Simple Sole

    1 pound fillet of sole
    Dash salt
    ½ cup light mayonnaise
    ½ cup light sour cream
    ½ cup grated Parmesan cheese
    Dash paprika
    Lemon wedges for garnish (optional)

Preheat the oven to 500°. Arrange the sole in a single layer in a greased baking dish. Sprinkle with dash of salt. Mix the mayonnaise, sour cream, and Parmesan cheese together and spread over the fillets. Sprinkle with the paprika. Bake for 10 to 12 minutes, until the fish flakes with a fork. Remove from the oven and let rest several minutes. Serve with lemon wedges, if desired.   Serves 4

NUTRITIONAL FACTS PER SERVING
Protein: 42 grams
Carbohydrates: 2 grams

Shrimp with Garlic and Wine Sauce

1 pound large shrimp
5 tablespoons olive oil
5 garlic cloves, crushed
2 tablespoons chopped parsley
1 teaspoon salt
2 tablespoons grated Parmesan cheese
3 tablespoons white wine
1 teaspoon pepper

Peel and devein the shrimp. Rinse quickly under running water. Heat the oil and sauté the garlic for about 2 minutes. Add the shrimp and parsley and cook gently on both sides for about 5 minutes. Season with salt and freshly ground pepper. Add the wine and stir well. Serve on hot plates. Sprinkle with Parmesan cheese.   Serves 4

NUTRITIONAL FACTS PER SERVING
Protein: 21 grams
Carbohydrates: 2 grams

Shrimp Catalina

1 pound fresh shrimp, boiled
2 large ripe tomatoes
1 stalk celery, chopped fine
½ teaspoon paprika
½ teaspoon salt
Light mayonnaise

Clean the shrimp and chill it. Peel the tomatoes, chop them fine, add the celery, and combine with the shrimp. Season with paprika and salt and add just enough mayonnaise to moisten. Mix well and serve cold on salad greens.   Serves 4

NUTRITIONAL FACTS PER SERVING
Protein: 24 grams
Carbohydrates: 4 grams

Salmon Supreme

¼ cup butter
Juice of 1 lemon
1 teaspoon Worcestershire sauce
½ teaspoon salt
¼ teaspoon paprika
½ teaspoon pepper
2 pounds salmon steaks
Minced parsley for garnish

In a shallow baking pan, melt the butter and then add the lemon juice, Worcestershire sauce, salt, paprika, and pepper. Coat the salmon in the butter and place the steaks side by side. Bake in a 400° oven for 15 minutes; turn the fish over and spoon some of the butter over the top. Bake about 15 minutes more, or until the fish flakes with a fork and is no longer translucent in the center. Serve sprinkled with parsley, if you like.   Serves 6

NUTRITIONAL FACTS PER SERVING
Protein: 24 grams
Carbohydrates: 1 gram

Salmon Fillets with Zinfandel Butter

¼ cup butter
¼ pound mushrooms, rinsed, dried, and sliced thin
¾ pound boneless, skinless salmon filet (cut into 6 equal-sized
   pieces)
Salt
Pepper
2 tablespoons finely diced shallots
⅔ cup Zinfandel
Chives, finely cut, for garnish

Melt 1 tablespoon of the butter in a 12-inch sauté pan over medium heat. Add the sliced and washed mushrooms and sauté until lightly browned, about 6 to 9 minutes. Remove from the pan, set aside, and keep warm. Add 1 tablespoon of the butter to the same pan and melt it. Add the salmon to the pan, season lightly with salt and pepper, and sauté until lightly browned, firm, and translucent at the thickest part (open or cut to test), about 7 to 10 minutes in all. Remove from the pan and keep warm. In the same sauté pan, combine the shallots and Zinfandel. Bring to a boil and boil, uncovered, until the mixture is reduced to about ¼ cup, about 4 minutes. Reduce heat to low. Add the remaining 2 tablespoons of soft butter, little by little, until it is melted and the sauce is smooth. Place the salmon on dinner plates. Top with the mushrooms, spoon the sauce over, and garnish with chives.   Serves 2

NUTRITIONAL FACTS PER SERVING
Protein: 28 grams
Carbohydrates: 4 grams

Fish with Cashew Nuts

2 tablespoons lemon juice
2 teaspoons grated lemon rind
6 fish fillets (favorite choice)
½ teaspoon salt
½ teaspoon pepper
½ cup flour
5 tablespoons olive oil
½ cup chopped cashew nuts
Parsley, minced, for garnish

Put the lemon juice and rind into a shallow dish and allow the fish to stand in the mixture for at least 15 minutes. Season fish with salt and pepper. Roll the fish in flour and fry in olive oil until tender. Remove the fish, set it aside, and in the same pan fry and lightly brown the cashew nuts. Serve the nuts over the fish, squeeze a little more lemon juice over the fish, and sprinkle with a little parsley.

                                        Serves 6

NUTRITIONAL FACTS PER SERVING
Protein: 28 grams
Carbohydrates: 2 grams

Red Snapper Veracruz Style

6 tablespoons olive oil
1 17-ounce can tomatoes, chopped
1 teaspoon Splenda
1 teaspoon chili powder
½ teaspoon allspice
1 garlic clove, crushed
Salt and pepper to taste
1 onion, finely chopped
6 red snapper fillets
1 4-ounce can pimientos, chopped
2 tablespoons capers, chopped
3 ounces pitted green olives, chopped

In a heavy skillet, heat 3 tablespoons of the oil. Combine the tomatoes with the Splenda, chili powder, allspice, garlic, salt, pepper, and onion and simmer in oil for about 10 minutes, covered. Coat the baking dish with the remaining oil. Put the fish into the dish; add the pimientos, capers, and olives to the tomato mixture and pour over the fish. Bake at 350° for 30 to 35 minutes, or until the fish flakes easily when pierced with a fork.

Serves 6

NUTRITIONAL FACTS PER SERVING
Protein: 28 grams
Carbohydrates: 4 grams

Ceviche

2½ cups lemon juice
1½ cups lime juice
1 tablespoon white pepper
1 tablespoon salt
1 tablespoon garlic granules
1 ounce Tabasco sauce
2 ounces safflower oil
5 pounds Pacific red snapper (cut into ½-inch cubes)
½ bunch green onions or scallions, diced
½ bunch fresh cilantro, chopped
1 medium bell pepper, diced

In a large bowl, combine the lemon juice and lime juice. Add the pepper, salt, garlic granules, Tabasco sauce, and safflower oil. Mix well. Add the snapper, onions, cilantro, and bell pepper. Gently mix well. Refrigerate for 12 hours to blend the flavors before serving. Serve on a chilled bed of lettuce with slices of lemon.   Serves 6

NUTRITIONAL FACTS PER SERVING
Protein: 20 grams
Carbohydrates: 4 grams

❖ ❖ ❖ **Vegetarian Protein Entrées** ❖ ❖ ❖

Oven-Baked Tofu

___

½ cup cracker crumbs, crushed fine
2 tablespoons cornmeal
½ teaspoon chili powder
½ teaspoon salt
1½ tablespoons of your favorite seasoning
    (Cajun, lemon pepper, etc.)
Sesame oil
1½ pounds (24 ounces) extra firm tofu, drained

Preheat the oven to 375°. Mix the cracker crumbs, cornmeal, chili powder, salt, and your favorite seasonings in a bowl and set aside. Lightly oil a large wire cooking or cooling rack. Cut the tofu into 12 sticks about 3 inches long and ¾ inch thick. Roll each stick in the crumb mixture and place on the wire cooking rack. Place the rack in the oven for 35 to 40 minutes, until crisp and brown. Serve with your choice of sauce on the side for dipping.

Serves 6 (24 sticks, 4 sticks per serving)

NUTRITIONAL FACTS PER SERVING
Protein: 28 grams
Carbohydrates: 3 grams

Soy Sausage Crustless Quiche

___

2 eggs or egg substitutes
1¾ cup milk (2% or skim) or soy milk
8 ounces soy sausage
½ cup broccoli, chopped
½ cup shredded reduced-fat Cheddar cheese or soy cheese

Preheat the oven to 425°. Combine the eggs and milk. Pour into a 9-inch glass pie dish. Crumble the soy sausage into the mixture along with the broccoli and cheese. Bake for 15 minutes. Reduce heat to 300° and continue to cook until set, approximately 30 minutes.   Serves 4

NUTRITIONAL FACTS PER SERVING
Protein: 21 grams
Carbohydrates: 8 grams

Mixed Fruit and Veggie Tofu Stir-Fry

1½ pounds (24 ounces) extra firm tofu, drained
2 tablespoons fresh ginger, grated
2 large garlic cloves, minced
3 tablespoons sesame oil
¼ pound broccoli florets
½ cup red pepper, slivered
½ cup yellow pepper, slivered
¼ cup roasted peanuts
1 cup mushrooms, sliced
1 8-ounce can pineapple chunks in juice, drained; reserve liquid
½ cup mandarin orange segments
¼ cup soy sauce
2 tablespoons tomato sauce
1 tablespoon cornstarch

Cut the tofu into ½-inch cubes. In a wok, sauté the garlic, ginger, and tofu in sesame oil until lightly browned. Remove the tofu and set aside. Add the broccoli, red pepper, yellow pepper, peanuts, mushrooms, pineapple, and oranges and stir-fry until the vegetables are tender-crisp. In a separate dish, combine the reserved pineapple liquid, soy sauce, tomato sauce, and cornstarch until smooth. Stir into the wok until all ingredients are well coated. Add the tofu cubes and serve hot.   Serves 6

NUTRITIONAL FACTS PER SERVING
Protein: 28 grams
Carbohydrates: 10 grams

Tofu Loaf

1 pound (16 ounces) extra firm tofu, mashed or crumbled
½ cup rolled oats
1 small onion, chopped
2 garlic cloves, minced
1 scoop (¼ cup) soy protein powder
¼ cup chopped fresh parsley
3 tablespoons soy sauce
½ teaspoon sage
½ teaspoon thyme
¼ cup catsup

Preheat the oven to 350°. Mix all the ingredients except the catsup in a bowl. Press the mix into an oiled loaf pan. Top with the catsup. Bake for about 30 minutes. Let cool for about 10 minutes before slicing.

Serves 8

NUTRITIONAL FACTS PER SERVING
Protein: 21 grams
Carbohydrates: 4 grams

Parmesan Tofu Cutlets

Olive oil
1 onion, chopped
2 cups tomato sauce
1 teaspoon garlic powder
1 teaspoon dried oregano
2 pounds (32 ounces) extra firm tofu, drained
½ cup egg substitute
¾ cup Italian seasoned bread crumbs
4 ounces reduced-fat mozzarella cheese, grated
4 ounces Parmesan cheese, grated

Preheat oven to 350°. Coat a large skillet with olive oil and sauté the onion until tender. Put the tomato sauce into a saucepan and add the onion and seasonings. Simmer for 15 minutes. Slice each pound of tofu into 4 lengthwise pieces (4 ounces each). Heat a medium skillet. Dip each tofu slice into the egg substitute, then coat with bread crumbs. Fry until delicately brown (approximately 3 to 4 minutes). Line a baking pan with a little sauce and layer in the cutlets, adding more sauce and some grated cheese between the layers. Save some cheese for sprinkling on top. Bake for 20 minutes.

Serves 8

NUTRITIONAL FACTS PER SERVING
Protein: 23 grams
Carbohydrates: 8 grams

Thai Vegetarian Stir-Fry

1 tablespoon peanut oil
1 pound (16 ounces) extra firm tofu
2 scallions
1 red bell pepper, cored and seeded
1 yellow bell pepper, cored and seeded
½ cup bottled Thai peanut sauce
½ cup peanuts, ground
2 tablespoons water

Cut the tofu into ½-inch cubes. Cut the scallions and peppers into 1-inch pieces. Heat the oil in a wok or skillet over high heat. Cook the peppers, tossing and stirring, for 30 seconds. Add the tofu cubes, tossing and stirring, for 1 minute. Add the peanut sauce and water, stirring until smooth and bubbling. Add the ground peanuts and scallions and reduce the heat to low. Cover and simmer for 10 minutes. Serve hot in bowls.   Serves 6

NUTRITIONAL FACTS PER SERVING
Protein: 21 grams
Carbohydrates: 5 grams

Vegetarian Burritos

2 tablespoons olive oil

1 pound (16 ounces) extra firm tofu, cut into ½ -inch cubes
(about 2 cups)

3 plum tomatoes, cut into ½ -inch cubes (about 1 cup)

2 small zucchini, halved lengthwise and cut into ¼-inch slices
(about 2 cups)

1 cup sliced mushrooms

1 small onion, cut into ¼-inch strips

1 teaspoon minced garlic

1 6-ounce can of tomato paste

¾ cup water

2 teaspoons chili powder

½ teaspoon hot pepper sauce

¼ teaspoon ground cumin

¼ teaspoon freshly ground black pepper

12 low-carbohydrate tortillas (see Appendix B)

Heat the oil in a large nonstick skillet over medium-high heat. Cut the tofu
and plum tomatoes into ½-inch cubes. Add the zucchini, mushrooms,
onion, and garlic. Cook, stirring occasionally, until the vegetables are tender, approximately 5 minutes. Combine the tomato paste, water, chili
powder, hot pepper sauce, cumin, and pepper in a small bowl; add the mixture to the skillet. Gently stir in the tofu cubes and plum tomatoes. Reduce
heat to low; cover and heat about 5 minutes. To serve, spoon about ½ cup
of mixture into each of the tortillas and roll them up.

Serves 6 (12 burritos, 2 burritos per serving)

NUTRITIONAL FACTS PER SERVING
Protein: 28 grams
Carbohydrates: 10 grams

VEGETABLE SIDE DISHES

Asparagus with Pine Nuts and Cheese

> 4 cups asparagus
> 4 tablespoons butter
> ½ cup pine nuts
> ½ cup Swiss cheese

Steam the asparagus until cooked and place in a warm serving dish. In a small pan, melt the butter and sauté ½ cup pine nuts for about 30 seconds. Pour the mixture over the asparagus and sprinkle with ½ cup shredded Swiss cheese.

Serves 4

NUTRITIONAL FACTS PER SERVING
Protein: 14 grams
Carbohydrates: 9 grams

Creole Green Beans

> 1 14½-ounce can stewed tomatoes
> 1 14½-ounce can green beans
> 1 onion, sliced
> 3 slices bacon, cooked until crisp and diced
> 1 tablespoon chili pepper
> Salt and pepper to taste

Mix all the ingredients together in a saucepan. Heat the saucepan over medium heat, stirring occasionally until vegetables are tender, approximately 5 minutes.

Serves 4

NUTRITIONAL FACTS PER SERVING
Protein: 1.5 grams
Carbohydrates: 8 grams

Mediterranean-Style Zucchini

4 tablespoons olive oil
1 large onion, minced
1 medium-sized garlic clove, peeled
1 stalk celery, minced or sliced thinly
½ green bell pepper, diced
¼ teaspoon oregano leaves, crumbled
6 small zucchini (about 1 pound), stem and blossom ends removed
Salt to taste

In a wide frying pan, combine the oil, onion, and garlic; cook, stirring occasionally, over moderately low heat until the onion is soft; do not brown. Add the celery, green pepper, and oregano and cook until just tender, stirring occasionally. Remove from heat and cover when cool. Split the zucchini lengthwise in halves. Drop into 2 quarts of rapidly boiling salted water and cook, uncovered, for 3 minutes after boiling resumes; drain. When ready to serve, add 3 tablespoons water to onion mixture and cook, stirring, over moderate heat until simmering. Add the zucchini and mix gently until heated. Salt to taste and remove the garlic, if you wish.

Serves 4

NUTRITIONAL FACTS PER SERVING
Protein: 0 grams
Carbohydrates: 8 grams

Hot Broccoli with Olive Nut Sauce

½ cup butter
½ cup slivered almonds
3 tablespoons lemon juice
1 clove garlic, crushed
1 2¼-ounce can sliced ripe olives, drained
3 pounds fresh broccoli, trimmed

Melt the butter in a small skillet. Add the almonds, lemon juice, garlic, and olives. Let stand 1 hour to blend the flavors. Reheat before serving. (May be refrigerated overnight and reheated.) Place the broccoli in a small amount of boiling water, cover, and cook until tender. Drain and place in a serving dish. Pour the sauce over and serve.   Serves 8

NUTRITIONAL FACTS PER SERVING
Protein: 1 gram
Carbohydrates: 10 grams

Savory Sauerkraut

1 medium-size onion, chopped
3 tablespoons bacon drippings
1-pound can sauerkraut, drained
1-pound can tomatoes
½ teaspoon caraway seeds
½ teaspoon Splenda

Preheat the oven to 350°. Fry the chopped onion in the bacon drippings until soft. Add the sauerkraut, tomatoes, caraway seeds, and Splenda; mix thoroughly. Turn into a 1½ quart casserole and bake uncovered for 30 to 40 minutes to blend the flavors.   Serves 6

NUTRITIONAL FACTS PER SERVING
Protein: 0 grams
Carbohydrates: 8 grams

Savory Sweet Peppers

3 red peppers (about 1 pound)
3 green peppers (about 1 pound)
2 tablespoons olive oil
1 tablespoon wine vinegar
½ teaspoon salt
½ teaspoon dried oregano leaves
⅛ teaspoon pepper

Wash the peppers. Cut each in half lengthwise and remove ribs and seeds. Cut each half in fourths lengthwise. Heat the oil in a large skillet. Add the peppers and cook over medium heat, stirring occasionally, for about 15 minutes, or until just tender. Gently stir in the vinegar, salt, oregano, and pepper.   Serves 6

NUTRITIONAL FACTS PER SERVING
Protein: o grams
Carbohydrates: 6 grams

Sicilian Broccoli

 1 bunch broccoli
 4 tablespoons butter
 2 garlic cloves
 ½ cup sliced black olives
 ½ cup chopped red bell pepper
 Parmesan cheese

Divide the broccoli into florets and steam until cooked. Place the florets in a warm serving dish. In a small pan, melt the butter, sauté the garlic, and add the olives and pepper. Pour the butter mixture over the broccoli and sprinkle with the cheese.   Serves 4

NUTRITIONAL FACTS PER SERVING
Protein: o grams
Carbohydrates: 5 grams

Stuffed Eggplant

1 large or 2 small eggplants
¼ cup butter
1 medium onion, chopped fine
1 green pepper, seeded and cubed
½ teaspoon salt
1 teaspoon basil
1 1-pound, (4-ounce can) tomatoes, drained
2 ounces processed Swiss cheese, cubed
½ cup pine nuts
Olive oil

Preheat the oven to 350°. Slice the eggplant lengthwise. Cut around egg-plant ¼ inch from edge. Carefully cut and scoop out the center, leaving a ¼-inch shell. Cube the center portion and set aside. Parboil the eggplant shell in boiling salted water for 5 minutes and drain. Melt the butter in skillet and add the onion, green pepper, and eggplant. Sauté until the veg-etables are tender. Add the salt, basil, tomatoes, cheese, and pine nuts; mix well. Spoon the mixture into the eggplant shell and place in a baking dish greased with olive oil. Cover and bake for 30 minutes or until the eggplant is tender. Cut into slices to serve.   Serves 4

NUTRITIONAL FACTS PER SERVING
Protein: 5 grams
Carbohydrates: 10 grams

DESSERTS

Note: Refer to Appendix B, "Recommended Products," for my top sugar-free syrup recommendations.

Sugar-Free Homemade Ice Cream

⅓ cup Splenda
1 cup whole milk
1 cup heavy cream
1 tablespoon sugar-free vanilla syrup

Mix the ingredients together, pour into the mixer of an electric ice cream maker, and follow the ice cream maker directions.

Note: Electric ice cream makers can be found in the kitchen appliance departments of all major department stores and specialty kitchen supply stores.   Serves 4

NUTRITIONAL FACTS PER SERVING
Protein: 3 grams
Carbohydrates: 2 grams

Sugar-Free Tapioca Pudding

3 tablespoons fine-grained tapioca
2 cups unsweetened soy milk
¾ cup sugar-free syrup (for example, almond, vanilla, caramel, chocolate)
3 to 6 single-serve packs of Splenda
1 egg or ¼ cup egg substitute

Place all the ingredients in a saucepan and let sit for five minutes, stirring occasionally. Bring to a full boil, over medium heat, stirring constantly. Remove from heat and allow to cool.   Serves 4

NUTRITIONAL FACTS PER SERVING
Protein: 5 grams
Carbohydrates: 5 grams

Sugar-Free Mousse

1 cup skim milk
1 envelope unflavored gelatin
½ cup powdered nonfat dry milk
¼ cup Splenda
1½ cups nonfat ricotta cheese
¼ cup cocoa
¼ cup sugar-free syrup (for example, caramel, vanilla, chocolate)
1 teaspoon vanilla extract
1 cup light whipped topping

Place ½ cup of the skim milk in a saucepan. Pour the unflavored gelatin in the milk and set aside for 2 minutes to allow the gelatin to soften. Place the gelatin mixture over low heat and cook, stirring constantly, for about 3 minutes, or until the gelatin is dissolved. Do not let the mixture boil. Remove from the heat and stir in the remaining ½ cup of milk, nonfat dry milk, and Splenda. Transfer the gelatin mixture into a mixing bowl and chill for 25 minutes. With an electric mixer, beat the chilled gelatin mixture at high speed until it is the consistency of fluffy whipped cream. Place the ricotta cheese, cocoa, sugar-free syrup, and vanilla extract in a blender and blend until smooth. Gently fold the ricotta mixture into the chilled gelatin mixture. Then fold in the whipped topping.

Divide the mousse into eight wineglasses. Chill for 2 hours. Top each with a tablespoon of light whipped topping and a sprinkle of cocoa.

Serves 8

NUTRITIONAL FACTS PER SERVING
Protein: 6 grams
Carbohydrates: 2 grams

Frozen Yogurt Pops

½ cup of your favorite fresh or frozen fruit (strawberries, peaches,
   blueberries, pineapple, cherries, raspberries)
1 cup plain low-fat yogurt
½ cup fruit-flavored sugar-free syrup (should match the fresh fruit)

Blend all the ingredients in a blender until smooth. Pour into Popsicle
molds and freeze.   Serves 4

NUTRITIONAL FACTS PER SERVING
Protein: 2 grams
Carbohydrates: 4 grams

Sugar-Free Fruit Parfait

1½ cups water
1 cup of your favorite fresh or frozen fruit (strawberries, peaches,
   blueberries, pineapple, cherries, raspberries)
1 packet unflavored gelatin
1½ cups seltzer
1 8-ounce package cream cheese
1 tablespoon fruit-flavored sugar-free syrup (should match the fresh
   fruit of choice)
½ pint of heavy whipping cream
¼ teaspoon sugar-free vanilla syrup
¼ teaspoon cream of tartar

If the fruit is larger, slice it; leave smaller fruits whole. Boil the water and
seltzer together and add the packet of unflavored gelatin. Stir the gelatin
until it dissolves and set aside 1 cup in the freezer for 30 minutes. Pour the
other 2 cups into 8 dessert dishes and place the dessert dishes in the refrigerator. Take the gelatin out of the freezer. Place the gelatin, 1 cup cream
cheese, 1 tablespoon fruit-flavored syrup, and 9 or 10 slices or pieces of the
fruit into a blender and blend for several seconds. Take the dessert dishes
and divide all but 16 of the fruit slices or pieces equally into the dessert
dishes. Next, pour the mix from the blender evenly into the dishes. Return
the dessert dishes to the refrigerator for 30 minutes. Pour the cream, vanilla

syrup, and cream of tartar into a large bowl. With an electric mixer, beat at high speed until it is the consistency of fluffy whipped cream. Take the dessert dishes out of the refrigerator and top with whipped cream mixture. Garnish with two fruit slices or pieces each.

NUTRITIONAL FACTS PER SERVING
Protein: 7 grams
Carbohydrates: 2 grams

Sugar-Free Cheese Pie

2 8-ounce packages fat-free cream cheese
2 tablespoons fat-free ricotta cheese
4 tablespoons of your favorite flavor of sugar-free syrup (vanilla, caramel, chocolate, lime, lemon)
½ cup Splenda
1 packet unflavored gelatin
1 cup boiling water

In a large bowl, soften the cream cheese and add the ricotta. With an electric mixer, beat at high speed until smooth and set aside. In a smaller bowl, mix the sugar-free syrup, Splenda, and gelatin. Add 1 cup of boiling water and stir until the gelatin dissolves. Add the ricotta and cream cheese mixture to the gelatin mixture and beat with the electric mixer at high speed until smooth. Pour into a 9-inch glass pie dish and refrigerate until firm (approximately 2 hours).   Serves 8

NUTRITIONAL FACTS PER SERVING
Protein: 6 grams
Carbohydrates: 2 grams

Appendix A: Commit to Health and Happiness

Here's one contract you won't have to run by an attorney. It's your own personal contract for health and happiness. Make a copy of this contract, sign it, and read it daily. Use it to reaffirm your desire and commitment to live in Total Health and renew your pledge to participate in life to the best of your abilities.

Remember, you have the right to be healthy and happy! It's my deepest wish that this book and the Total Health program will help you take the first steps toward lifelong good health and happiness.

𝕿otal 𝕳ealth

Contract for Health & Happiness

I, _____ , hereby declare that I promise myself and my loved ones to nourish my body with a proper diet and to enjoy the lifelong benefits of physical and mental health through exercise, intellectual development, and spiritual growth.

This commitment will help me maintain and enjoy the quality of life that I most certainly deserve for participating in life to the best of my abilities.

Signed:_____ Date:_____

Appendix B: Recommended Products

Fiber, vitamin and mineral supplements
Holland & Barrett
0870 606 6606
Web site: www.hollandandbarrett.com

Health 4 You
Web site: www.health4youonline.com

Protein products
Creatine Store Ltd.
68 Wood Street
Liverpool
L1 4DQ
0870 240 7687
Web site: www.creatinestore.com

Low Carb products
Megastore UK
Unit 142
Leyland Trading Estate
Irthlingborough Road
Wellingborough
Northants NN8 1RT
01933 279069
Web site: www.lowcarbmegastore.com

Carblife On Line Ltd
Unit 1
Capenhurst Technology Park
Chester
Cheshire CH1 6EH
0840 770 3070
Web site: www.carblife.co.uk

Sugar-free products
Sugar Free Superstore Ltd
PO Box 6818
Kettering
Northants NN15 7WS
0845 226 0624
Web site: www.sugarfreesuperstore.co.uk

Bibliography

Anderson, Bob. *Stretching.* Bolinas Calif.: Shelter Publications, 1984.

Agatston, Arthur. *The South Beach Diet: The Delicious, Doctor-Designed, Foolproof Plan for Fast and Healthy Weight Loss.* New York: Rodale Books, 2003.

Alpers, D., R. E. Clouse, and W. F. Stenson, eds. *Manual of Nutritional Therapeutics,* 2nd ed. Boston: Little, Brown, 1998.

Atkins, Robert. *Dr. Atkins' New Diet Revolution.* New York: M. Evans and Company, 1999.

Audette, Ray, with Troy Gilchrist. *Neanderthin: Eat like a Caveman to Achieve a Lean, Strong, Healthy Body.* New York: St. Martin's Press, 1999.

Break Free of Junk Food and Sugar Cravings—for Life! New York: Harper-Collins, 1997.

Brzycki, Matt, ed. *Maximize Your Training: Insights from Leading Strength and Fitness Professionals.* Chicago: Masters Press, 2000.

D'Adamo, Peter, with Catherine Whitney. *Eat Right for Your Type: The Individualized Diet Solution to Staying Healthy, Living Longer and Achieving Your Ideal Weight.* New York: G. P. Putnam, 1996.

Daoust, Joyce, and Gene Daoust. *40-30-30 Fat Burning Nutrition: The Dietary Hormonal Connection to Permanent Weight Loss and Better Health.* Del Mar, Calif.: Wharton Publishing, 1996.

Dufty, William. *Sugar Blues.* New York: Warner Books, 1976.

Eades, Michael, and Mary Eades. *Protein Power.* New York: Bantam Books, 1996.

Encyclopedia of Foods. San Diego: Academic Press, 2002.

Erasmus, Udo. *Fats and Oils: The Complete Guide to Fats and Oils in Health and Nutrition.* Vancouver: Alive Books, 1986.

Gittleman, Ann. *The 40-30-30 Phenomenon: The Easy-to-Follow Diet Plan*

Tailored for Individual Needs. New Canaan, Conn.: Keats Publishing, 1997.

Guyton, Arthur. *Textbook of Medical Physiology,* 7th ed. Philadelphia: W. B. Saunders, 1986.

Haas, Robert. *Eat to Win: The Sports Nutrition Bible.* New York: Rawson Associates, 1983.

Hecker, Arthur, ed. *Clinics in Sports Medicine: Nutritional Aspects of Exercise.* Philadelphia: W. B. Saunders Company, 1984.

Heller, Richard, and Rachael Heller. *The Carbohydrate Addict's Diet: The Lifelong Solution to Yo-Yo Dieting.* New York: Penguin, 1991.

———. *Carbohydrate-Addicted Kids: Help Your Child or Teen Break Free of Junk Food and Sugar Cravings—for Life.* Diane Publishing Company, 1997.

Lemon, P. W. "Effects of Exercise on Dietary Protein Requirements." *International Journal of Sports Nutrition* 8 (1998): 426–427.

Neporent, Liz, and Suzanne Schlosberg. *Weight Training for Dummies.* New York: IDG Books Worldwide, 1997.

Poortmans, R., and O. Dellaliux O. "Do Regular High-Protein Diets Have Potential Health Risk on Healthy Kidney Functions in Athletes?" *International Journal of Sports Nutrition and Exercise and Metabolism* 10, no. 1 (2000): 28–38.

Sears, Barry, with Bill Lawren. *The Zone: A Dietary Road Map to Lose Weight Permanently, Reset Your Genetic Code, Prevent Disease, Achieve Maximum Physical Performance, Enhance Mental Productivity.* New York: ReganBooks, 1995.

Sizer, Frances, and Eleanor Whitney. *Nutrition: Concepts and Controversies,* 6th ed. St. Paul, Minn: West Publishing Company, 1994.

U.S. Food and Nutrition Board. *Recommended Dietary Allowances.* Washington, D.C.: National Academy Press, 1989.

Vigilante, Kevin, and Mary Flynn. *Low-Fat Lies: High Fat Frauds and the Healthiest Diet in the World.* Washington, D.C.: Lifeline Press, 1999.

Weil, Andrew. *Eating Well for Optimum Health: The Essential Guide to Food, Diet, and Nutrition.* New York: Alfred A. Knopf, 2000.

———. *Natural Health, Natural Medicine: A Comprehensive Manual for Wellness and Self-Care.* New York: Houghton Mifflin, 1995.

Zarins, Bertram, ed. *Clinics in Sports Medicine: Olympic Sports Medicine.* Philadelphia: W. B. Saunders, 1983.

Index